Twayne's English Authors Series

EDITOR OF THIS VOLUME

Kinley E. Roby

Northeastern University

Josephine Tey

TEAS 277

JOSEPHINE TEY

By SANDRA ROY

TWAYNE PUBLISHERS
A DIVISION OF G. K. HALL & CO., BOSTON

Published in 1980 by Twayne Publishers,
A Division of G. K. Hall & Co.
All Rights Reserved

Printed on permanent/durable acid-free paper and bound
in the United States of America

Frontispiece artwork courtesy of Verlag L. Däbritz,
Alleinvertrag ART H. Hilscher, Munich

Library of Congress Cataloging in Publication Data

Roy, Sandra.
Josephine Tey.

(Twayne's English authors series ; TEAS 277)
Bibliography: p. 189–95
Includes index.
1. Mackintosh, Elizabeth, 1896–1952—
Criticism and interpretation.   I. Title.
PR6025.A2547Z87   823'.9'12   79–17585
ISBN 0–8057–6776–2

Contents

About the Author

Sandra F. Roy is a counselor of children and adolescents in Aiken, South Carolina. She also teaches on the graduate level at the University of South Carolina at Aiken. Dr. Roy holds the B.A. degree from Elmhurst College, the M.A. degree in creative writing from Ohio University and the Ph.D degree in Early Childhood from the University of South Carolina at Columbia. She has authored several texts for college level literature courses as well as numerous poems and short stories. Her interest in detective fiction is one of long standing and she has designed a course of study in the history and development of detective and mystery fiction.

Preface

Elizabeth Mackintosh is known primarily for the novels written under the pseudonym of Josephine Tey. She was also in her day a popular dramatist, novelist, and historical biographer under the name of Gordon Daviot. Her most successful play, for example, *Richard of Bordeaux,* was produced by and starred Sir John Gielgud. It is for her dramatic works that Miss Mackintosh wished to be remembered. Scornful of her detective fiction, she considered herself an historical writer whose plays and novels would finally reveal the ultimate truth concerning historical events and personalities. Aside from her many dramas, Miss Mackintosh wrote three non-detective novels, *Kif, Expensive Halo,* and *The Privateer* as well as a biography of John Graham, *Claverhouse,* all of which will be briefly considered here. Ironically, only her detective novels remain in print and available to the public. It is hoped that *Kif* and *The Privateer,* two of her best works, will be reissued in the near future under the more familiar Tey pseudonym.

Josephine Tey's mystery novels have gained in popularity since her death in 1952, and it is on these that this study will concentrate. Since Miss Tey began writing in the midst of the "Golden Age" of detective literature, her work reflects both the traditional approaches seen in the early Agatha Christie and Dorothy L. Sayers, as well as the later techniques espoused by Raymond Chandler and Dashiell Hammett. This study will consider the various devices, techniques, and approaches garnered from these two types. Stressing style and emphasizing characterization, Tey bridges the gap between the classic mysteries of the 1920s and 1930s and the "hard-boiled dick" of World War II vintage.

Tey's first novel, *Man in the Queue,* and her second, *A Shilling for Candles,* reflect the traditional plot. Her third novel, *Miss Pym Disposes,* is closer to the tradition of the spinster detective such as Agatha Christie's Jane Marple or Patricia Highsmith's Miss Silver. *The Franchise Affair,* her fourth mystery novel, is a rewriting of the historic Canning case in modern terms in which a young girl accuses two women of kidnapping, beating, and imprisoning her. In Tey's fifth novel, *Brat Farrar*, a criminal becomes the detective. *To Love and Be Wise*, Tey's sixth novel, deals with transvestitism and fraud, an unusual combination for detective fiction. *The Daughter of Time*, undoubtedly Tey's most famous and popular novel, illustrates the similarities between the approach of detective and scholar and is a novel of dramatic suspense with absolutely no action. Tey's final novel, *The Singing Sands*, returns in some respects to her first works and is a traditional detective novel.

While Tey's plotting varies from the pedestrian to pedantically brilliant, her flair for characterization develops steadily. This study will trace that development as well as the author's use of such theatrical devices as foreshadowing, dialogue, suspense, and denouement. Though not a brilliant writer, Tey deserves close scrutiny for her careful, workmanlike approach to characterization and her ability to create realistic and memorable major as well as minor characters. Special attention will be paid to Tey's development of unique detectives whose self-torturing consciences plague them into moral judgments which are often contrary to the law.

While stressing the author's able characterization, this study will not ignore her intricate counterpoint of symbol and theme. Her symbology is approached in terms of ironic physical and thematic psychological symbols. The author's reiterative, compulsive, and disturbing major themes of deception, mistaken identity, and isolation are focused on both to elucidate her works and to illuminate her own carefully hidden personality and philosophies.

Finally, it should be noted that there has been no significant criticism of either the Tey novels or the Daviot works. Tey, in spite of her masterly characterization and compelling themes, is largely ignored in the traditional studies of detective fiction. Nor have there been critical articles, with the exception of the usual book reviews. Since Tey, whose popularity daily increases, wrote in the august company of Agatha Christie, Dorothy L. Sayers, Margery Allingham, and Ngaio Marsh, and can be compared favorably with them, she should no longer be ignored.

My work in gathering material, collating information, and

Preface

writing analyses was greatly helped by the kind patience, tolerance, forgiveness, and help of my husband, Dr. Emil Roy. To him, great thanks and the return of his typewriter.

SANDRA ROY

University of South Carolina, Aiken

Chronology

1897   Elizabeth Mackintosh born in Inverness, Scotland, exact date unknown.

1918   (approximately) Graduated from Anstey Physical Training College, Birmingham, England.

1926   (approximately) Retired as physical training instructor and returned to Scotland to care for an invalid father.

1929   As Gordon Daviot published *Man in the Queue* and *Kif.*

1931   As Gordon Daviot published *Expensive Halo.*

1932   First production of *Richard of Bordeaux* in London.

1933   Publication of *Richard of Bordeaux* under the Daviot pseudonym.

1934   *The Laughing Woman* and *Queen of Scots* produced at the New Theatre.

1936   *A Shilling for Candles* published under the Tey pseudonym.

1937   *Claverhouse* published under the Daviot pseudonym.

1939   *The Stars Bow Down* published under the Daviot pseudonym.

1941   *Leith Sands* performed as a radio drama.

1946   *Leith Sands and other Short Plays* published under the Daviot pseudonym; *The Little Dry Thorn* performed in April at Citizens Theatre in Glasgow.

1947   *Miss Pym Disposes* published under the Tey pseudonym.

1949   *The Franchise Affair* and *Brat Farrar*, both published under the Tey name.

1950   *To Love and Be Wise* published under the Tey name.

1951   *The Daughter of Time* published under the Tey pseudonym.

1952   Died in Scotland, February 13.

1952   *The Singing Sands* published under the Tey pseudonym; *The Privateer* published under the Daviot name.

1953–   *Plays by Gordon Daviot*—a three volume work.
1954

CHAPTER 1

Life and Works

JOSEPHINE Tey and Gordon Daviot were the two pseudonyms used by dramatist and novelist Elizabeth Mackintosh. Miss Mackintosh was born in Inverness, Scotland, in 1897. The exact date of her birth, like many other pertinent facts concerning her life, is not known. Educated in the town of her birth, she attended the Royal Academy.

Destined for a university, I stuck my toes in and refused to continue what I had been doing for the previous twelve years. I balked too, at art—my talent is on the shady side of mediocre—and settled for a course in physical culture and have never regretted it. I trained at the Anstey Physical Training College in Birmingham for three years and have earned my living all over England as a physical training instructor.[1]

No doubt her experiences at Anstey were used as background for *Miss Pym Disposes* (1947) which is set at Leys Physical Training College.

For eight years Miss Mackintosh followed her profession, resigning finally in the mid 1920s to care for her invalid father near Loch Ness and to pursue a writing career. She became a full-time writer with the publication in 1929 of her first detective novel, *The Man in the Queue*, written under the name Gordon Daviot. (It was later republished using the Tey pseudonym.) Her first play accepted for production was *Richard of Bordeaux* (1932), and it is for her plays that she wished to be remembered. She says as much in the information provided for the 1948 *Who's Who*, mentioning first *Richard*, and continuing:

Other plays: *The Laughing Woman*, produced 1934; Queen of Scots, 1934, both at the New Theatre; *The Little Dry Thorn*, Citizens Theatre, Glasgow, April 1946. Publications: three novels, the best known being *Kif; Claverhouse* (biography) 1937; *The Stars Bow Down*

13

(play), 1939; *Leith Sands* (one-act plays), 1946. Radio *Leith Sands* (play) 1941. Writes detective stories under the name of Josephine Tey novels.[2]

Richard of Bordeaux ran for fourteen months in 1932 and 1933 in London and starred Sir John Gielgud who became acquainted with "Gordon Daviot" during the production. He describes her as ". . .a strange character, proud without being arrogant, and obstinate though not conceited."[3] She often refused to rewrite plays, preferring nonproduction to change. On the few occasions when she did rewrite, as in *Queen of Scots*, she implied that the play's lack of success was caused primarily by the alterations. Gielgud insists that "she was distressed by her inability to write original plots, especially when, on two occasions she was unfairly accused of plagiarism" (p.ix). This may account for her heavy reliance on historical sources for both plays and novels.

Shy to the point of phobia, she had few intimate friends and confided in no one. Seldom visiting London, she, unlike so many writers, was not anxious for actors or producers to read her plays, and she loathed and refused to read them aloud herself. Shunning publicity completely, Miss Mackintosh gave no press interviews.

Surprisingly, her interests lay not in the theater but in the film. The influence of motion pictures is apparent in many of her works, in particular *The Privateer,* her last novel. She went to the cinema twice a week and enjoyed discussing action, direction, and film techniques, topics she carefully avoided when discussing drama. Her other few amusements included horse-racing and "country," which probably included, if her novels are any guide, fishing in the streams of Scotland.

The works written under the Daviot name were without doubt her favorites, yet only *The Man in the Queue,* reissued under the Tey pseudonym, remains in print. Miss Mackintosh cared little for the Tey books, referring to them as her "yearly knitting" (p. x).

The first Tey novel, *A Shilling for Candles,* appeared in 1936 to mixed reviews. It must be remembered, however, that the competition was fairly stiff with Dorothy L. Sayers, Agatha Christie, and Margery Allingham publishing prolifically, to name only a few. In this so-called "Golden Age," the most popular form of detective fiction was that of the involved puzzle solved by the clever and witty amateur sleuth.

The Tey pseudonym was then abandoned temporarily in favor of the Daviot plays. In 1947, Miss Mackintosh returned to mystery fiction and "began to use as an alias the name of my Suffolk great-great-grandmother, Josephine Tey."[4] *Miss Pym Disposes*, the only Tey novel to use a Jane Marple-type detective was quickly followed in 1949 by *Brat Farrar* and *The Franchise Affair*, both dealing with charming, amoral criminals. *To Love and Be Wise* appeared in 1950, and the most popular and well-known Tey novel *The Daughter of Time* was issued in 1951, a few weeks before her death. Miss Mackintosh had known herself to be fatally ill for over a year and had avoided seeing any friends or acquaintances, preferring to suffer quietly and alone. Gielgud states "this gallant behavior was typical of her and curiously touching if a little inhuman too."[5] She died in London at the age of fifty-five. Two of her works were published posthumously, *The Singing Sands* and *The Privateer*, both in 1952, along with a three-volume collection of her plays in 1953.

I *Inferences*

Of her personal life, we know practically nothing, aside from an assumption by Gielgud that she suffered a personal tragedy in World War I and in 1942 was very depressed and unhappy. One might assume that the latter too was in some way connected with a war, although there is no way to know definitely. The author never spoke of her feelings, ambitions, or desires, although it is possible that some of her sentiments and inclinations are revealed in the process of her art. If this is so, the reader can at least make a few basic assumptions about Mackintosh and her personal relationships. Most obviously, though it is more apparent in the Daviot plays than the Tey novels, she had a fascination for historical characters, settings, and action. The past was exciting, stimulating, and filled with real individuals, not the cardboard reflections so many of us imagine.

Second, although her dislike and distrust of those who advertise themselves as Christians is blatantly apparent, she was nonetheless well-read in the Bible as evidenced in many plays, those dramatizations of biblical events as well as other works in which the Bible is often quoted.

That she distrusted actors is also obvious. Marta Hallard,

Grant's acquaintance in the Tey novels, is usually cool, remote, callous, and self-centered, yet at times sensitive and intuitive. Tey revealed her opinions of the theatrical world in devastating caricature in *To Love and Be Wise.*

Who, then, did she trust? Quite obviously, until 1949 at least, the answer is children, in particular clever teen-age girls. They are witty and, to the author, always right in their character judgments. The young ingenues in *A Shilling for Candles, Brat Farrar,* and *Miss Pym Disposes* are some of her most memorable and likable characters. In *The Franchise Affair,* however, the young teen-ager turns betrayer; she lies, indulges in illicit sexual activities, and is totally self-oriented, even a bit stupid. After this denunciation, a teen-ager does not again figure significantly in any of the works.

Miss Mackintosh herself had difficulties establishing close ties with others. Consequently none of her characters experience a significant male/female relationship. Grant must be the loneliest of all detectives without a close friend, confidant, wife, or girl friend. Only in *The Privateer,* published in 1952 after her death, does she draw a character who has close friends and is emotionally involved with their fates. Henry Morgan, in fact, seems to have a plethora of close friends—Bart, Mansfield, Speirdyck, Morris, and Modyford. Most of his adventures result from a resolve to avenge the death of a friend. Undoubtedly Miss Mackintosh's approaching death colored her writings, and she was expressing a desire for just such friendships. Perhaps in her reticent Scots manner, she was protesting her own early death at the age of 55.

Certainly the author's outstanding trait was her maternal instinct. In many of her plays and most of her novels, the heroes are men who need comfort and protection—who are innocent and sometimes even boyish and romantic. The women act first and always as mothers, reassuring, feeding, bolstering weakened self-confidence. Ideally, they understand men intuitively and can and should anticipate their every need. For all this effort, their reward is, if it happens at all, a brief smile at best. In *To Love and Be Wise,* for example, Marta tells Grant:

You feel that way only because you are tired and hungry; and probably suffering from dyspepsia, anyhow, after having to eat at the White Hart for two days. I'm going to leave you with the sherry decanter and go down and get the wine . . . When I've brought the wine up from the cellar I'm going to cook you an omelet as only I can cook one, and then we'll settle down.[6]

A more extreme example is Mary in *Expensive Halo*. Mother of a large family, married to a self-righteous brute, she suffers and endures all for husband and children, anticipating and granting if possible their desires. Was this the sort of woman the author saw in Josephine Horne Mackintosh, her mother? Undoubtedly she exhibited many of these traits.

And finally, what of fathers? Miss Mackintosh nursed her invalid father for many years, which must have strongly influenced her. Yet, oddly enough, father figures are not common in her works. When they do appear, they are treated with a mixture of fear, some tolerance, and a little contempt. Grant's chief is known to be irascible and irritable, to be approached only when in a pipe-smoking good mood. Alfred, the father in *Expensive Halo,* was self-righteous, cruel, bigoted, selfish, and egotistical. Certainly not the best of men, but nonetheless the most memorable character in the novel.

Finally, one somehow feels obliged to inquire about the author's world view. If the themes of her writings can serve as a guide, and they are the only guide available, Miss Mackintosh saw life as deceptive, unreliable, and emotionally dangerous. It is foolish, she says, to believe in anything or anyone for nothing is what it seems. The guilty are usually innocent as in *The Man in a Queue;* the wise, foolish; and the obvious deduction inevitably wrong. Appearances are generally deceiving. A brother is not a brother but a cousin, a man is not a man but a woman, an innocent girl is in fact a nasty-minded trollop. It is no wonder then, that Miss Mackintosh seldom ventured far from Inverness and that she so thoroughly enjoyed films where all is obviously pretence and falsehood. It must have been reassuring for her.

II   *The Plays*

Before proceeding with the study of the works of Elizabeth Mackintosh, it is necessary to divide them by types, partly for the convenience of classifying according to definition and partly to illustrate the author's immense diversity and talent.

Unknown to readers of the Tey novels, Miss Mackintosh was an

extremely prolific playwright under the pseudonym of Gordon
Daviot. From 1930 or 1931 until her death two decades later, she
wrote over a dozen full-length dramas, and an equal number of
one-act plays. At the outset of her career as a dramatist, she
managed to interest Sir John Gielgud in producing and acting in
Richard of Bordeaux in 1932. The play enjoyed a fourteen-
month run in London. The success was due in part to Daviot's
somewhat unique approach to history. Always conservative, she
presented her heroes and heroines as middle-of-the-roaders.
Neither terrible nor perfect, they usually exhibited some sense
of humor and constancy in the face of crisis. She could not
portray a cruelly wanton Mary of Scotland nor a wicked Richard
III.

Her *The Laughing Woman* opened April 7, 1934. Daviot left
the theater as suddenly as she had embraced it, only to pour
prodigious efforts into plays that received provincial or radio
productions at best. A volume of short plays appeared in 1946,
followed by a series of three collections published posthumously
from her papers: in 1953, 1954, and an undated volume a year or
so later. Daviot's favorite topics for dramatization were biblical
and English history, and her central figures were aristocrats,
politicians, military leaders, or artists with clouded reputations.
She preferred unified plot lines and dealt with family groups set
within interior box sets. Writing consistently in idiomatic English
prose, she relied on rather flat and conventional types for
supporting characters with a tendency toward muted conflicts
and stagy conclusions. Her dramas illustrate the author's ease of
characterization, her ability to translate the abstract, occasionally banal characters into living beings with realistic
personalities and idiosyncrasies.

III   *Non-Mystery Works*

Next, and even less well known than the dramas, are the four
non-mystery/detective works including three novels, *Kif, Expensive Halo,* and *The Privateer,* and one biography, *Claverhouse.*
Kif, published in 1929, the same year as *The Man in the Queue,* is
by far the superior novel. Its style could loosely be termed
psychological. The action traces the experiences of a malad-
justed teen-ager in the first World War, his unsuccessful
attempts to deal with civilian life and his own emotions, and his

final, unwitting descent into crime and death by hanging. Reminiscent of Joseph Conrad's *Lord Jim, Kif* deals with a boy who can control neither his environment nor himself and comes to a sorry, inevitable end. The emphasis of the novel is one of character rather than action, an approach modified and used later in the detective novels.

It is difficult to believe that the author of *Kif* also wrote *Expensive Halo*. Far from a psychological novel, *Expensive Halo* is a romance written according to the well-worn standard; rich boy meets poor girl, boy loses girl, boy gets girl, with variations on the theme. Daviot has two sets of lovers, a wealthy man and his sister who fall in love with a poor but honest and talented brother and sister. With more humor, the novel would have been a parody of the traditional love story. Proving to herself and her public that this mode was characteristically incompatible with her temperament, Daviot then abandoned once and for all any attempts to make emotional attachment the central theme of a novel.

Her third work is again entirely different from the others. Once again the reader encounters Daviot the historian-scholar. *Claverhouse* is the biography of John Graham of Claverhouse, a Scottish soldier and tactician who led the Scottish rebellion against William of Orange in the name of James II. That the author's research was carefully detailed cannot be denied, but her tendency to reform and perhaps even whitewash her favorite rogues often obscures historical reality. Claverhouse was undoubtedly not as cruel as his enemies portrayed him, but it is unlikely that he was as good, kind, forgiving, clever, and diplomatic as Daviot portrays him. Claverhouse seems more the result of research for a drama or novel than a separately thought out biography.

Finally, among the non-detective works is *The Privateer*, a posthumously published adventure story in the tradition of Sir Walter Scott. While character is traditionally central, action runs a close second. This is, in fact, the only work in the author's canon that contains almost constant, exciting, dramatic action. Historical in orientation, *The Privateer* is the story of Sir Henry Morgan and his rise from bondsman to privateer (some insist buccaneer) and knighthood. Daviot is careful to distinguish between piracy and privateering, the latter being to the average observer merely a legalized version of the former. It is unfortunate that the author did not live to continue writing the action-adventure novel, since she apparently discovered a satisfactory form for non-detective works.

CHAPTER 2

Theatrical Successes

I The Early Theatrical Successes

MISS Mackintosh clearly contemplated a career as a serious dramatist on the London stage as she wrote a series of four full-length plays in the early 1930s. Making consistent use of the Gordon Daviot pseudonym, she completed *Richard of Bordeaux* (1932), *The Laughing Woman* (1934), *Queen of Scots* (1934), and *The Stars Bow Down* (1935). All of the plays but *Laughing Woman* were based on historical or biblical sources; all but *The Stars Bow Down* received full-scale productions.

Richard of Bordeaux (1932) deals with a series of crucial incidents in the life of Richard II. First seen in 1385, at the age of nineteen, Richard is pressing an unpopular peace with France upon baronial factions led by Gloucester. Angered by the destruction of his favorite, Robert de Vere, and helpless in the power of Gloucester, who controls Parliament, Richard asserts his majority at the age of twenty-three and placates Lancaster with a title. At the moment of a celebration of peace with France, his beloved Anne dies.

Still secretly nursing his desire to avenge de Vere, Richard engineers the deaths of Gloucester and Arundel and marries the infant daughter of Charles VI of France. Assuming that his power is unrivalled, having packed Parliament with his own supporters, Richard takes advantage of a quarrel between Mowbray and Henry, Earl of Derby, to send them both into exile: Mowbray is sent away for life as a long-deferred vengeance on the man for his previous enmity to de Vere.

The balance of power abruptly shifts as the Archbishop of Canterbury invites Henry, now Duke of Lancaster, back to England to regain his estates confiscated by Richard and to take the throne. Richard finds himself powerless and isolated, left with no choice but forced abdication.

Richard of Bordeaux closely follows historical accounts of one of England's less successful kings. Gordon Daviot artfully handles a succession of incidents and personages which leave an impression of tactful regret, "if only it could have been otherwise." Her panoramic scenes are all interiors which subtly emphasize the conflicts of tenderness, impulse, and cruelty beneath Richard's tenacious struggle for survival, even when he is physically absent from the stage. Whatever their ambitions, Daviot's characters are uniformly reasonable, well-spoken, and understated whether in prosperity or defeat. Daviot's themes seem quite consistent: the superiority of an unpopular peace to self-defeating warfare, the perseverance of personal loyalties beneath the appearances of political expediency, the tendency of thrusts toward vengeance greed, and personal triumphs to break through moderation and good sense. The author's sympathies seem quite royalist and paternalistic, with barely concealed hostility toward democratic and fraternal ideals. Behind the plans of ambitious men work unseen the inexorable forces of a shaping historical vitality.

The Laughing Woman was first produced on April 7, 1934, two months before Queen of Scots, although Gielgud does not recall seeing the former play until 1936. The title refers to a bust modelled after the Swedish mistress of Daviot's protagonist, a young and talented French artist named René Latour. The play portrays the course of their relationship from their initial meeting in Paris, their decision to leave for England and life in poverty as "brother and sister," followed by the gradual absorption of his mistress's talents in René's growing mastery of his craft. After two years together, just as René has completed a number of brilliant drawings and statuary, war breaks out, and René returns to France and a battlefield death. The play's prologue and epilogue set "at the present day" reveal the now aged Ingrid Rydman, once René's mistress, seated near her lover's laughing, youthful bust of her.

The Laughing Woman is singular among Daviot's early full-length plays for its modern and unhistorical theme. In terms reminiscent of D.H. Lawrence, the author mismatches a high-minded and fairly reserved Northerner with a passionately direct Mediterranean. Their relationship is chaste and male-dominated, unlike Sons and Lovers, with a fairly predictable melodramatic ending. Daviot's group portraits of London artistes, their patrons and parasites are drawn with a fresh verve and comic malice. Although the conclusion of her play dips into the pathos Gielgud faulted later in *The Stars Bow Down,* Daviot reveals an unsuspected talent for crisp and tersely written romantic comedy.

Queen of Scots (1934) follows *Richard* closely with another confused and impulsive royal failure from the Elizabethan period. Daviot introduces Mary at the age of eighteen in 1561 when her dynastic ambitions to displace Elizabeth led to her subsequent impulsive marriage to Henry Stuart, Lord Darnley. From the ensuing seventeen-year period ending with Mary's departure from Scotland to plead for Elizabeth's protection, the author selects the most dramatic crises of the Scottish queen's career. After the spoiled Darnley connives at the murder of Mary's capable Italian secretary Rizzio, Mary countenances a plot to destroy her husband by a group of conspirators. She then runs off with a leader of the plot, James, Earl of Bothwell. Having lost public support and standing condemned in the eyes of her people for murder and adultery, Mary undergoes a forced abdication, makes her escape from Edinburgh, and is finally forced from Scotland following Bothwell's defeat at the hands of Mary's brother James.

Even more than *Richard,* Daviot's third play suggests the influence of George Bernard Shaw and Sean O'Casey. She manages an artful mingling of commoner and aristocrat with authentic idioms proper to each. And her characters are strongly portrayed, though with a characteristic tendency to talk out rather than act out their passions, pushing violence offstage or leaving it to report. With some notable exceptions, conflict is muffled. We hear about Mary's brother's and courtiers' objections to Darnley, are told about Knox's confrontation with the Queen, and hear the briefest comment on the final disastrous battlefield defeat. Daviot's characters develop powerful personal loyalties, exhibit convincing rationales for their actions, and never slip into bawdy or curses. In his notes on the play John Gielgud tactfully remarks that "the results" of his suggestions for revision "were not equally successful" with those for *Richard.* In fact, Daviot shares one distinct trait with her characters: it was "hard to draw her out." On balance, however, *Queen of Scots* remains a subtle and meticulously crafted drama worthy of a stage or television revival.

In *The Stars Bow Down* (1935) Daviot closely follows the biblical story of Joseph and his brothers, basing the title on her hero's famous dream in which the sun, moon, and eleven stars (one for each brother) bowed down to him. Yusef's (Joseph's) life is portrayed from adolescence when he is sold into slavery by his jealous brothers, is purchased by Potiphar at an Egyptian market, and rises quickly to become his master's highly efficient steward. At the height of his rise, Yusef is wrongly accused of rape by Potiphar's wife and is imprisoned, only to be released and taken to the Pharaoh to interpret the great leader's dream of the seven fat and seven lean cattle. Named by the grateful Pharaoh as his second in command, Yusef supervises Egypt's management of the grain supply through plenty and famine, cleverly undercuts an attack by his father-in-law, Egypt's high priest, and reconciles himself with his brothers.

Daviot has continued to mine historical veins with *The Stars Bow Down*, while returning to biblical matter of interest to British dramatists since the Mystery plays. Her conventions are drawn from the well-made play in her use of the successive rises and falls of fortune endured by her hero, stock characters such as the Pharaoh as doddering Senex ("old man"), the intriguing priest as biter-bit, the seductive siren, and country-boy-makes-good. Her mastery of dialogue which catches individual nuances of character is impressive, although the action proceeds in an even more leisurely way than that in her earlier two full-length plays. She attributes the play's failure to gain a production to unwillingness to stagger "with imitative gestures in the footsteps of genius," fearing that unfavorable parallels would be drawn between her play and a recent production of Sir James Barrie's *David* play. Daviot's deep interest in historical themes was linked in her mind to what Gielgud terms "her inability to write original plots," adding that she had been sued by the author of an historical novel about Richard the Second. Although the case was settled out of court, suggesting some degree of culpability on Daviot's part, the experience seems to have added to her shyness and spikiness. Daviot's consistent use of prose in her dramas, while T.S. Eliot and W.H. Auden were attempting to reintroduce verse into the theater, reflects an interest in films which far outran her involvement with legitimate theater, which she seldom saw.

II   *The Interim Short Plays*

After twelve years' absence from the stage, quite possibly

prompted by charges of plagiarism and the unlucky coincidence of the production of James Barrie's *David* play just after the completion of *The Stars Bow Down*, Daviot published a thin volume of eight one-act plays (1946). The first of these, *Leith Sands*, is set in a Scottish sea town tavern in 1705 where a law student named Duncan Forbes condemns the hanging of Captain Thomas Green and several of his crew for the murder of Sandy Craig and the piratical pillaging of Craig's ship, the *Speedy Return*. The executions were based on hearsay and perjury, pumped up by the Scottish animus against England, Forbes claims. The play closes with the return of Craig from the "dead" to vindicate the wrongly executed Green. Daviot's use of the trial mode within the tavern followed by a surprise reversal is a neat use of the courtroom conventions of detective fiction. The play also reveals her fondness for the rehabilitation of scoundrels which appears repeatedly in her fiction, notably *The Daughter of Time*.

Rahab, like *The Stars Bow Down*, draws on Old Testament materials. During the siege of Jericho, Rahab hides two Israelite spies, gaining in return their promise of safety after the walls tumble and the town is sacked. The motif of pure prostitute redeemed by religious fervor, along with the theme of urban iniquity swept away by desert-hardened asceticism, are deftly handled.

Daviot sets *The Mother of Masé* in Thebes around 1500 B.C. The play adopts a biblical theme again, this time the relationship between Moses (Masé) and the Egyptian princess Hetshepsut whose Jewish maid Yaheb "found" him among the reeds fifteen years before. Like the Joseph of *The Stars Bow Down*, Moses is spoiled and immature. His discovery of his Hebrew parentage, cancelling out his heritage of Egyptian princeliness, coincides with Miriam's revelation that he is to lead his people from Egypt. His departure for battle against the Nubians as an assertion of masculinity repeats René Latour's irrational return to a country he had previously maligned. And in common with *Stars*, the play utilizes a *bildungsroman* or "development of a young man" theme with its revelations of unsuspected kinship and interwoven portents of the future.

Sara is yet another biblical play, revolving around the fears of Abraham's family that his sanity is slipping. It is set in about 2000 B.C. in Ur which a mysterious Voice has told Abraham to leave, taking his entire extended family with him. While the plot itself is remarkable, the play deals again with a yearning for a simple alternative to competing faiths and ideologies. It is also effective in handling the tensions within a family group that is paradoxically tied to and weary of one another. The unfinished quality of the play may have induced Daviot to take it up later as the first act of *The Little Dry Thorn* (published seven years hence in 1953).

Mrs. Fry Has a Visitor combines the novelties of a mid-nineteenth-century setting and a feminist theme: the dedication of the Quaker Mrs. Fry to prison reform. The action of the play focuses on the desire of a young woman to find a cause and use its power to break away from her family, much as the prim Swedish woman philosopher in *The Laughing Woman* personifies a devotion to art in her lover René Latour. One may also detect in Mrs. Fry's musings the views of her creator that a career has great rewards not necessarily including happiness, that the greatest satisfaction of all would be in the love of one's children (denied both character and creator), and that the greatest temptation of public acclaim is vanity. The characteristic last-minute revelation of identity, that the Young Lady seeking Mrs. Fry's advice is Florence Nightingale, is stagy and unconvincing, failing to redeem the pedestrian talkiness of the play.

Three Mrs. Madderleys brings together rather chancily the newly divorced second wife, first wife, and mother of John Madderly, who comes alive in their reminiscence. Each discovers that John had manipulated her by idealized praise of an earlier woman in his life stretching all the way back to his perfect "nanny." The play unconsciously dramatizes the Freudian myth that some deeply wounded men pursue the perfect mother through an unending series of surrogates. In a final touch of irony, not only John's wives but his mother find themselves outclassed by his Nanny and, ultimately, exorcise their own imagined shortcomings. In short, the play dramatizes the means by which each of one man's women finds her own proper role and the self-esteem to make them bearable.

Clarion Call centers about the reuniting of lost son with his family by the newspaper of the title. The action largely concerns the hostility and indifference felt toward each other by a jaded and mercenary young man and his carping, disappointed mother before they part again. Unfortunately, Daviot endows her characters with neither charm nor interest.

Remember Caesar invokes the Restoration England of Charles II. Lord Weston who serves as one of the King's judges finds the scrawled note in his pocket, notes the date as March fifteenth, and is immediately overwhelmed by assassination fears. In perhaps the masterpiece of the volume, Daviot anatomizes the comic efforts of an obsessed ditherer to avoid a totally imaginary threat on his life. The denouement identifies Mr. Caesar of the note as a man who has come to see Weston's rose trees.

The short plays in this volume are typical of Daviot's taste for a wide range of comic types, a gift for witty Shavian riposte, and a weakness for neat and stagy curtains. She also is a shrewd and telling observer of hypocritical and impersonal institutions and deception. Her one-acts make economical uses of box sets and small casts while she manages a nearly seamless blend of historical verisimilitude with timeless humorous foibles.

III   *The First Posthumous Collection of Plays*

One of three posthumous collections of full-length plays was published in 1953, including *The Little Dry Thorn, Valerius,* and *Dickon.* Since no production records accompany the plays, though Daviot provides her future director with suggestions regarding setting and characterization, the plays were presumably written between 1946 and the author's death in 1952. *The Little Dry Thorn* extends the earlier one-act *Sara* by tracing the intertwined fortunes of Abraham, his wife Sara, his handmaiden Hagar, and his brother Lot, along with the latter's doomed wife Milcah. The literal action details Abraham's search for the Promised Land, his taking of Hagar to his bed and the resulting product of their union, the malicious Ishmael, followed by Sara's "miraculous" pregnancy and Hagar's expulsion after her plot against the infant Isaac is discovered and foiled. Beneath this rather rambling and slow-moving narrative emerges a modern double triangle. Abraham's barren, though loving marriage to Sara is complicated by Sara's brokerage of a union between her husband and handmaiden Hagar. She herself achieves a winter pregnancy (it is suggested) with the willing connivance of her husband's steward Larsa—a benign version of the Potiphar's wife story Daviot had earlier included in *The Stars Bow Down.* The play's quotient of tension is fairly mild: Milcah turns salt-colored in a bath of burning oil, Hagar and Ishmael are sent into the desert with a pension after a bungled attempt to kill Sara's child with a poisonous spider while the miraculous child results from an extramarital liaison. Compared with the leaps into faith of T.S. Eliot's and Christopher Fry's religious plays, the Daviot play dips into rationalism and melodrama.

Valerius is a two-act dramatization of a besieged Roman garrison in Caledonia at the end of the second century A.D. In the course of the play, the Romans are surrounded and cut off by the savage Caledonians in their isolated northern fort. Their leader Valerius sends out messengers for help from the Legion in York as their rations dwindle and their numbers drop from the fighting and sickness. The heaviest blow to Valerius, however, is the death of his beloved friend Rufus from an arrow wound. The Legion finally arrives, summoned by a friendly Caledonian trader, and Valerius assumes command of the effort to rebuild the wall which was destroyed by the enemy.

The play reveals the same interest in historic and, specifically, Scottish themes which appear in works such as *Queen of Scots*. The Romans are vivid stock types from the stalwart captain Valerius, to his faithful companion Rufus, the rabble-rouser malcontent Varus, and the distinguishable "flat" characters which add color and interest to the play. Daviot's Romans speak a slightly heightened, though idiomatic English which is terse and crisp sounding. And she manages the illusion of suspense and violent action through her careful use of timing and the vivid reporting of offstage action. Interestingly enough, in this highly competent effort, no woman ever appears, and biblical echoes are absent.

Dickon (1943), like the Tey novel *The Daughter of Time* (1951), deals in two acts with Richard III of England and takes much the same approach, as her extensive historical notes indicate at the end of the play. She treats the last two and a half years of Richard's life extending from just before the death of Gloucester's brother Edward IV to the morning of his fateful battle with the invading forces of Henry Tudor from France. The play dramatizes "Dickon's" firm but compassionate suppression of Edward's wife's relatives, the Woodvilles, through the failed rebellion and capture of his trusted but envious friend Buckingham. By the end of the play, which covers roughly the same historical span and most of the incidents of the Shakespearean version, Richard emerges as an enlightened though beleaguered statesman, a loving husband and father, and a victim of political instability. He finally falls through unprincipled betrayal: "But for the treachery of one man (Stanley)," Daviot writes in her notes, "Richard III would have won the battle of Bosworth, and the venomous hunch-backed monster who appears in the pages of Tudor historians would never have been invented."[1]

In *Dickon,* Daviot has crafted a smooth and appealing drama which relies upon her impressive historical research into original and subsequent authorities. She manages in her play and notes to demolish "calumnies" such as Richard's hump and withered arm; his murder of Edward, Henry IV's son, of Henry VI, and his own brother Clarence; his usurpation and subsequent tyranny; and his murder of his nephews in the Tower. These revisions of the popular view are effectively woven into the play. In this respect, *Dickon* fits the Daviot penchant for rehabilitating rogues who are destroyed by the ambition of friends and the excitable stupidity of mobs. The dramatic tension and clashes of strong will, unfortunately, are sacrificed as well; the play will live, if at all, as popularized history rather than as theater.

While it is impossible to place these plays either by order of composition or even to date them within the six-year period following the 1946 publication of her short plays, they are consistent with the subjects and themes of her earlier dramas. The Bible and English history, though pushed back to the Romans in *Valerius,* are drawn upon. Her central characters are leaders saddened by the loss of friends, defeated by unthinking opposition, and misunderstood by history. Except for *The Little Dry Thorn,* which focuses on the powerful personality of the biblical Sara, the plays relegate women to minor roles or omit them entirely. And Daviot's interest has shifted from youthful to middle-aged characters, perhaps consistent with her own process of aging.

IV   *The Second Posthumous Volume of Plays*

Yet a second volume of plays by Gordon Daviot was published posthumously in 1954. It included three full-length plays, *The Pomp of Mr. Pomfret, Cornelia,* and *Patria,* along with three one-act plays, *The Balwhinnie Bomb, The Pen of My Aunt,* and *The Princess Who Liked Cherry Pie.*

The Pomp of Mr. Pomfret dramatizes an elaborate practical

joke perpetrated on the vain, pompous politician of the title. Two assorted couples meet initially in an exclusive restaurant: John Judd, millionaire builder from Canada, and Donald Macallister, a newspaperman, and Valenti and Rose, brother and sister who perform acts of magic in nightclubs. When the restauranteur moves them out at Pomfret's demand, they join in a plot to embarrass and humiliate the M.P. Rosa gains employment as a maid in Pomfret's home and, by the tricks of her trade, makes a flower jug hurl itself at her head. She sues and wins. Acting as a kind of "Duke of dark corners," Judd has secretly bought up Macallister's newspaper, insuring that Pomfret receives enough unwelcome notoriety to drive him out of Parliament and into retirement. Daviot reveals an obvious zest for farcical mischance and trickery, a love of jokes that deflate self-important clowns, and an enduring interest in probing the insecurities that lie beneath brittle impersonations. Her true metier in the theater may have lain in broad farce.

Cornelia is a three-act romantic comedy based rather loosely on Bernard Shaw's *Pygmalion* and Christopher Fry's *Venus Observed*. After her father's death, Cornelia leaves Labrador to join her father's one-time employer, Lucas Bilke. She quickly demonstrates enormous skill at golfing, shooting, and fishing while captivating Bilke, a spoiled and titled neighborhood liberal named Sebastian Binnacle, and Bilke's butler Parkins. She finally marries the butler and takes him back to Labrador to share the running of a hotel with her. *Cornelia* is the wittiest and most appealing play Daviot wrote since her one-act *Remember Caesar*. Each of the characters has pomposities to be punctured and obsessions to be teased away. Cornelia is artless and direct, one of Daviot's best portraits of the captivating naïf and ingenue. The play belongs to the best tradition of English comedy stretching back to Congreve and Sheridan and fully deserves a production.

Patria is an allegorical drama regarding the attempts of a small group of nationalists to free the mythic Creeland from the Tainian empire. A clique calling themselves the Patria adopts a native costume. By pointing to an ancient battle lost to the Tainians in 1349, they manage to win a municipal election. When they approach the emperor to ask his blessing on their establishment of a Free State, he agrees but on one condition: that the five leaders of the independence movement never take office of any kind in Creeland. Their announcement of this condition to their countrymen is met by derision, and the movement collapses. The play glances at past and ongoing civil crises in Ireland, Ulster, and Scotland, to say nothing of Wales and other more distant parts of the British Empire. Daviot's use of figures such as the Wastrel, the Poet, the Merchant, and others, drains the play of any warmth or empathy. She presumably would have preferred to leave it unpublished.

The Balwhinnie Bomb dramatizes in one act the discovery in the small post office of Balwhinnie of a bomb addressed to visiting royalty. After the postman, Roddy Ross, returns from an unsuccessful job-seeking trip to London, he and the postmistress, Anabella Morrison, find the suspicious ticking parcel. Roddy opens it, and the local policeman dismantles the bomb. A phone call to the monarch bring the promise of a decoration for Roddy. However, a sharp-eyed shoe repairman recognizes his own figuring on the bomb's wrapping paper, exposing Roddy as the culprit: he had hoped through his ruse to gain recognition. This deftly managed little farce is fast-paced and suspenseful. Its concluding twist reveals some typical Daviot themes. There is the obscure, but ambitious nobody who dreams of glory, the attempted impersonations, and the last-minute stripping away of ignorance: "No mortal in fact is free of the god's laughter," she remarks in a note, "however free he may be of worldly failings."[2]

The Pen of My Aunt portrays the encounter of a lady in occupied France with a German corporal who is seeking the identity of a wandering stranger. She pretends with her maid Simone's help that he is her nephew and that, unfortunately, his identity papers had been sent to the laundry with his coat. The lady is also able to suggest a resting place for the fugitive, who is heading for the coast and freedom, and browbeats the corporal into giving him a ride. "The Pen" of the title refers to a hiding place for a list of members of the resistance that the supposed "collaborator" of the title is keeping. It is a carefully crafted, if dated, short play, marked by a sustained high pitch of interest and lively dialogue.

The Princess Who Liked Cherry Pie is a charming little children's play. In order to gain the hand of the Princess Greensleeves, a series of four suitors must guess the answer to a riddle: how do turnips grow? One after another fails until Ping-Pong wins. The wedding is jeopardized when he admits he does

not like the Princess's favorite dessert, cherry pie: too many
stones. However, the problem is resolved by a page whose father
was gardener to a magician; he can grow cherries without stones.
The play is fairy-tale-like in its simplicity and humor.

While it is difficult to generalize about the development of
Daviot's craft as a dramatist in this volume, subjects drawn from
the Bible or past English history are absent. Her fondness for
aristocrats, politicians, and soldiers is present in all these plays;
and all but *Patria* provide women with leading roles. All are
wryly or good-humoredly comic with detailed stage directions,
revealing Daviot's continued interest in stage productions.

V   *The Third and Final Posthumous Volume of Plays*

The last volume of Daviot's plays published after her death
includes three full-length plays: *Lady Charing is Cross, Sweet
Coz*, and *Reckoning*, along with two short plays, *Barnharrow* and
The Staff Room. Except for *Barnharrow*, they are all set in the
present century and combine a love interest with politics,
religion, education, or a career. And each of them centers around
the stripping away of illusion from a passionate, if confused,
central female figure.

Lady Charing Is Cross is a romantic comedy reversing the
Pygmalion motif Daviot had treated earlier in *Cornelia*. The play
has two levels, political and social. On the political level, Lady
Charing, who runs the most exclusive salon in London, is
persuaded to invite a new socialist M.P. from Kilcrannock to tea
in order to "take the rough off him." She succeeds so well that he
changes his dress, his politics, and his party. By the end of the
play he has become a Liberal clearly destined for the Prime
Ministry as a Conservative. On the social level, Lady Charing
becomes intrigued and then deeply involved emotionally with
the young man, Neil Tummel, first in love with him and then out
again—hence the "cross" of the title. It becomes clear that he
has finally become his own man and no longer Lady Charing's
creation. The play works a mild variation on Daviot's repeated
theme of whitewashing a rogue. Tummel changes from an
insincere poseur pretending to be working class into the
ambitious, winning politician he had been at heart all along.
Daviot's language is taut and comic; her repartee never flags or
slips into flatness. The play occasionally seems dated and

confined to a now-extinct social class, but retains great interest.

Sweet Coz dramatizes in three acts the day after a chance meeting between a very straight female doctor and a drifting though talented architect posing as her cousin. The plot is a slim one. The doctor's brother Hector, a poet and pampered journalist, becomes persuaded that the architect is a genius and has designed exactly the house for his lady love, who is a wealthy and doting widow. The visitor fairly guilelessly reveals to the doctor that Hector is a pompous and self-centered ass, much as the magicians had deflated Mr. Pomfret in *The Pomp of Mr. Pomfret*. Hector takes himself angrily away after he and his sister have stripped away one another's pretensions. The field is left to the architect and the doctor who will undoubtedly make a match of it. *Sweet Coz* is a rather fluffy and pleasant little farce devoid of malice. As in *The Mother of Masé* and *The Three Mrs. Madderleys,* a pampered and childish young man is torn away from female overprotection, while a roguish interloper emerges as a master of benevolent manipulation, a magician with words like Joseph in *The Stars Bow Down* and Valenti in *Mr. Pomfret.*

Reckoning closely resembles an American 1930s type of gangster film complete with low-life criminals, a hopeless love affair, and a tearful ending. A beautiful young girl named Nell falls in love with a burglar named Ted Hanna. Despite her better instincts and the cautions of her uncle, Mr. Biddle, she goes off to live with him. When she is unable to reform him, she tolerates his continued burgling. After more than a year of marriage, however, he confesses he has killed a man in the course of a robbery, using a gun belonging to a mutual friend, Fluff Williams, who is arrested for the crime. Fluff accepts blame for the killing and is executed, largely because of his warm feelings for Nell. Angry and disillusioned by the life of lies her love for Ned has forced her into, she shoots him and prepares to end her own life. The play is slow and talky, notable largely for subject matter close to the Tey novels and the films she loved. The stagy dialogue and claustrophobic setting are authentic, although the violence of strong emotion is lacking.

Barnhallow is set in Scotland of the 1680s when religious conflicts were smouldering. Daviot centers her play around Janet Linton, Rob Linton, her father-in-law, and her Covenanter son Simon and niece Ishbel Grierson. After her son returns from an illegal conventicle where Patrick Kennedy is raising an army to

attack the King's forces in a religious war, Janet learns that her
son has shot the Anglican minister, Mr. Pierce. Simon had
assumed—wrongly—that it was Pierce who had reported the
conventicle. The issues raised in the play are too remote in time
and too parochial to have great force as dramatic conflict.
However, the tensions they involve within a rural Scottish family
are vivid and gripping.

The Staff Room dramatizes the impact of the visit of an
Inspector of Schools, Mr. Woodington Smith on the staff of a
girls' high school. It turns out that Smith had known the teacher
of physical education previously when she had cared for him in a
hospital. They go to lunch together. It is a slight play little more
eventful than its synopsis.

Daviot's sustained energy in the creation of drama is as notable
as her connection with the Tey novels is unknown. Over a period
of two decades, she created over two dozen short and full-length
plays. From an artistic point of view her difficulties with plotting
are balanced by her interest in biblical and historical actions.
Her characters are fairly stock, and conflict rarely if ever bursts
through her tightly controlled societies and highly capable
prose. Although she probably would have preferred that a few of
her plays never see print, she never gave up hope that her drama
would receive thoughtful productions from sensitive production
companies.

CHAPTER 3

The Others

MACKINTOSH wrote three novels that were not mysteries under the Daviot pseudonym, and one biography. The works were not enthusiastically reviewed and have long been out of print. In the case of *Kif: An Unvarnished History*, this is regrettable. *Kif* was published in 1929, the same year as *The Man in the Queue,* though it was to all intents and purposes ignored in favor of the mystery novel. Perhaps readers were bored with novels about the impact of war on an individual, or perhaps the "unvarnished history" was too familiar and painful a reality. Nonetheless, with the increased interest in both World War I and its effects on the British citizenry in particular, there is little doubt that *Kif* would prove popular today, both as a novel and as a dramatization akin to those being done of the works of Somerset Maugham and John Galsworthy.

I Kif

The action begins in 1914 when Kif, a fifteen year-old orphaned farm worker enlists. His motive, unlike most of the British public, was not patriotism, but a painful desire for adventure. He wanted to experience something new, exciting, and even dangerous each day, and the army certainly fulfilled these demands. Naive, innocent, and simple, Kif takes an almost childish delight in seeing London on leave. Once in France, he enjoys the hardships of the trenches with the same simplistic excitement. He makes several friends among the troops: one of them, Tim Barclay, is from a reputable and wealthy London family. Kif spends a leave with the Barclays and is intrigued by Ann, Tim's sister, though he is too shy, frightened, and insecure to approach her. In fact, none of Kif's relationships with women are truly successful; even his friendships with the men show a

35

reticence and restraint. In the Sómme offensive, Kif is wounded
and sees several of his friends die. While he is recovering,
Barclay decides to take a commission, leaving Kif bereft of all his
friends. This is the first of three successive betrayals by Barclay
who lacks the moral courage to be firm and accept responsibility.
Back in camp, Kif meets Thomas Carroll ("Angel") who will
ultimately lead Kif to destruction.

After the war, Kif returns to London with fine hopes for the
future. These are slowly ground to dust. He cannot get any job he
likes. Finally he invests his savings in a bookmaking business, and
things go well temporarily. He enjoys visiting the race tracks and
for a time even considers buying his own horse. His decision to
visit the Barclays once again, Ann in particular, heralds the
beginning of his downfall. He is received coldly, much to his
disappointment. He had naively assumed their friendliness was
sincere and that their hospitality was meant for him as a person,
not just a soldier friend of Tim's. Disappointed and angry, Kif
asks Tim to visit him at his office. As he later discovers, Tim did
visit, but then did not pursue the friendship. A few months later,
one of his partners absconds with all the money, leaving Kif poor,
jobless, and bitter. Racing is now forever closed to him.

In December, he meets Carroll again—fortuitously, since he is
nearly ill of starvation and cold. Carroll takes Kif home with him
and offers him bed and board, both gratefully accepted. Carroll's
sister, Baba, an uninhibited flirt, plays with Kif's emotions. The
family is well on the wrong side of the law, and Kif joins them
while he courts and adores Baba. Taking part in a burglary with
Carroll's father, Kif is caught and sentenced to prison. The worst
of being incarcerated was, to Kif, the interminable boredom. By
now his innocence is somewhat tarnished, but he nonetheless
believes that his "friends" are basically "decent." Once released,
he attempts to make an honest living, but finds that impossible
for an ex-convict. Returning to his life of crime, he shoots a man
in self-defense during a burglary and is sentenced to death.
Neither Tim nor Baba, two of the people he ultimately loved,
would visit him. Only Ann, now married to Kif's commanding
officer in the army, insists on daily visits. To her, Kif is "a brick."
Yet, the only person who weeps over his death is Mary who
worked with him on the farm and used to give him extra tea and
candle ends so that he could read.

In *Kif*, Daviot first presents the theme of honest rogue. This character appears frequently in her non-detective works and dramas. Surprisingly, he is used only in *Brat Farrar* and *The Daughter of Time* among the canon of eight mystery novels. This theme obviously aroused some deep and ambivalent feelings in the author.

Essentially, her approach is the same, whether dealing with Richard the Third or the unknown Kif. The central character (in this case *hero* is a most appropriate term) has a catalogue of admirable virtues—honesty, integrity, cleverness, sincerity, etc., in addition to one foible. In the case of Kif, it is his desire for adventure; Richard's is softheartedness regarding the Woodvilles. Obviously, these are scarcely severe drawbacks. Nonetheless, they inevitably bring about the temporary, if not permanent downfall of the individual. Daviot takes pains to point out that, while her hero may seem a criminal to most observers, he is either the victim of circumstance as Kif or Brat, or a misjudged combination of Daniel and Robin Hood, serving justice and good government against the wicked rebels. Their actions should not only be pardoned but praised, the author implies. Ironically, of the historical characters she attempted to vindicate, only Harry Morgan the privateer was officially recognized by his government as performing a useful and valuable function, being knighted as a reward.

Undoubtedly *Kif* deserves both reissue and careful study. As a psychological novel it fits neatly into the mainstream of literature between Joseph Conrad and Somerset Maugham. Kif, unable to control outer reality, is equally incapable of dealing with his inner tensions and conflicts. His quests for adventure, excitement, and understanding lead inevitably to an early death. Ironically, like most young men in modern literature, his quest is basically directionless. The reader can see its purpose and aim, but the questor himself is unaware of his goal.

II Expensive Halo

Daviot's second traditional novel, *Expensive Halo*, is a disappointment. One expects more than a trite plot, absurd characters, unbelievable motivation, and mechanical action from the author of *The Man in the Queue* and *Kif*. Published in 1931, *Expensive Halo* is a "woman's novel" in the pejorative sense. Full of improbable love affairs, a self-sacrificing mother, a spurned sweetheart, and a cruel father, the book resembles the bastard offspring of a literary coupling of P.G. Wodehouse and "The Perils of Pauline."

The novel consists basically of three pairs of characters. Mary Ellis and her husband Alfred are the ghosts of Christmas future, so to speak. Their far-from-ideal marriage involves Mary in continual capitulation which will inevitably recur in the lives of her children. Mary is the noble, long-suffering, sorely tried "MOTHER," enduring the self-righteous bullying of her husband, a part-time preacher and a full-time unscrupulous greengrocer.

Alfred Ellis is a man of God, a fanatical sectarian whose overt piety conceals a vicious avariciousness and a violent, unmanageable temper. His bungling attempts to interfere in the lives of his children make the early chapters of this book far superior to the remainder of the story.[1]

Gareth, Mary's favorite son, is a talented violinist, naive and unselfconscious (though by no means a genius). A favorite character type of Daviot's, particularly in the dramas, Gareth needs continual reassurance, bolstering, and attention. Needless to say, a long line of women is willing to inflate his ego. Although engaged to Molly, the girl next door, who can always deal with his erratic moods, he falls desperately in love with Ursula Deane. The latter is a motiveless, bored, impulsive society girl reminiscent of a less amusing Dorothy L. Sayers character. In *Murder Must Advertise* (1933) the society dilettante is perfectly portrayed by Sayers in the character of Dian de Momerie. Unfortunately, Ursula more closely approaches a flat caricature. Meanwhile, unknown to Ursula, her brother, a notorious "sport" and playboy, has fallen in love with a dressmaker, Sara Ellis, who, by the strangest of coincidences, is Gareth's sister. Handled by playwrights WilliamWycherley or William Congreve, the complications might have been far more witty and amusing.

After a good deal of tears, frustration, and fury, Sara persuades Ursula to turn Gareth away and return him to Molly "who is good for him." Although insisting (somewhat mechanically) that she is in love for the first time, the wealthy socialite agrees. She then decamps for a cruise in the Aegean as a distraction. Sara and Ursula's brother, Chitterne, now reformed, will fulfill the dream of rich man/poor girl and wed, making future family parties a bit

awkward. The reviewer for the *New York Times* aptly describes
the novel's shortcomings:

> Her heroes and heroines, rich and poor, are straw-stuffed marionettes
> whose speeches are a credit to the author's literary ventriloquism
> rather than to her ability to create authentic conversation. Even the
> noble Ursula, whose renunciation supplies the expensive halo of the
> title, is a character fashioned with scant understanding. Handicapped
> by a stilted plot and unavoidable mechanical characters, Miss Daviot's
> second novel falls short of her initial effort.[2]

Yet, there is no doubt that the writing of *Expensive Halo* was
practical and instructive. On the one hand, Daviot discovered
that the love story was not her strong suit. However, she also
discovered both the virtues and the pitfalls of the doubling motif,
while handling the intricacies of balanced and opposing characters. These devices were used successfully later in *Brat Farrar*
where brothers and sisters interact in an atmosphere of dramatic
tension lacking in *Expensive Halo*.

III   Claverhouse

Daviot's fascination with historical characters first emerged
with the 1932 production of *Richard of Bordeaux*, foreshadowing the extremely successful *The Daughter of Time* which is
concerned with the vindication of Richard III. Having used
history as a basis for both fiction and drama, the author naturally
turned to biography as well. In 1937, Gordon Daviot published
her study of John Graham of Claverhouse. It was not a success,
and she never again attempted straight biographical work.

Claverhouse covers a period of Scottish history from 1648 to
approximately 1689, focusing on the life of John Graham,
undoubtedly as unfamiliar to most Americans as to professional
historians. A peg for every unpleasant legend according to
Daviot, Claverhouse was the eldest son of a conservative family
related to the Stewarts. When Charles returned to England,
young Claverhouse at age twelve was made a burgess of the town
of Dundee. Little is apparently known of his personal life, though
the author makes character estimations based on various
paintings—a favorite pastime of Inspector Grant in *The Daughter of Time*. Ultimately Dundee, as Claverhouse is called,

becomes a soldier and officer and is sent by Charles II to deal with the Covenanters in Scotland. Like so many others, his battles against the rebels are inconclusive. According to Daviot, Dundee was not guilty of the cruelty and murderous acts with which he is apparently credited by tradition. Further, she suggests, the fact that he chose a life of responsibility and risk in the service of the king is to his credit. With his handsome manners and appearance, he could easily have been a successful court "climber."

Put in charge of several "difficult" counties, Claverhouse governs them well, proving an expert in common sense and jurisprudence. His success makes him enemies among the King's men as well as in the dissenting kirk which encouraged discontent, rebellion, and hatred.

That is to say that any one who hated a man to the point of a "call" had only to indulge his hatred. He ran the risk of being hanged, of course, if caught, but if that happened he was a martyr (in most cases a "saint") and his comrades would avenge him. So much for the Church of Christ in Scotland![3]

Tey's dislike and even hatred of the Convenanters is apparent on every page. The kirk foments trouble whenever possible, and lies whenever necessary, creating martyrs of hoodlums, murders, and rebels. (In *The Daughter of Time* Tey applies the term "tonypandy" to events that are reported as historically accurate, but which never took place, such as the martrydom of most Covenanters.) Daviot further insists that Dundee's reputation for slaughter as recorded by Daniel Defoe, Thomas Macaulay, and Sir Walter Scott is pure calumny. A true loyalist, Dundee killed only two people, both criminals and, the author suggests, deserving death. Daviot takes great pains to present her hero as reasonable, diplomatic, and clever with admirable leadership abilities. They are the same traits, incidentally, with which she credited Richard III and Henry Morgan.

When James is exiled, Dundee escapes to the Scottish Highlands to gather friends and troops for the king. His clan support is brave and colorful, but untrained and more inclined to loot than battle if the opportunity presented itself. In a battle against superior troops at Killiecrankie, the Highlanders win, but Dundee is killed and the rebellion dies with him.

This biography's lack of public appeal is perhaps obvious. While the whole world has heard of Richard III, few individuals are aware of the existence, let alone significance, of John Graham of Claverhouse. Though obviously well researched, the style lacks the polish and balance usually associated with Daviot. Her foreshadowing, for example, is a heavy-handed attempt at sustaining interest where there is none. Finally, American readers will find the historical background obscure. English history before, during, and after Cromwell is difficult to follow at best. And Scottish history, influenced so thoroughly by England and the rebelling Covenanters, is nearly impossible without a detailed chronology.

IV   The Privateer

The Privateer (1952), Daviot's final non-mystery, is, like *Kif* and *Claverhouse,* the study of a rogue. According to most accounts, Henry Morgan was an accomplished pirate; Daviot of course disagrees. Using historical information as thoroughly as in *Claverhouse,* she creates a fictionalized biography that is far more successful.

Morgan, a freed bondsman in Barbados, joins with a group of "traders" and captures a Spanish ship. Rather than turning it over to the English government and Cromwell's man, Morgan decides to keep it for his own and ransom crew and passengers. Leaving his prisoners in Tortuga, he returns to Barbadoes to learn that Cromwell is dead and political feelings toward Spain are changing. The governor, Sir Thomas Modyford, is most reluctant to deal with the Spanish prisoners.

Teaming up with Jack Morris and his crew, Morgan becomes a self-styled privateer. That is, he has no official government sanction for his attacks on Spanish ships and is in effect a pirate. Daviot insists that since Morgan's motives were more concerned with destroying the hated Spanish than with personal gain, he was not in fact a pirate. The distinction is scarcely visible to the reader [and the captured Spanish ships alike.]

After obtaining a ship for Morris by capturing a likely looking Spanish ship, the captains learn that privateers are being recalled. England is now allied with Spain. Furthermore, and much to their delight, Morris and Morgan learn that Morgan's uncle is now governor of Jamaica. Arriving with three Spanish "prizes," the captain is shocked to discover his uncle dead; Modyford, the unsympathetic governor of Barbados, is now in charge.

Visiting his uncle's family, Morgan falls in love with his cousin Elizabeth at first sight and spends his share of the prize money buying a plantation. Meanwhile, Morgan, Morris, Captain Mansfield, and others prepare an expedition against the Dutch, England's current enemy. Once the ships near Curaçao, however, the men refuse to fight, partly because the Dutch have always been friendly, and partly because they were such excellent sailors and soldiers. The crews insist on capturing the Spanish island of Santa Catalina instead. The "impossible" island is taken easily and without loss of life since the Spaniards prefer to cut and run.

Henry returns to Port Royal and marries Elizabeth only to discover on his wedding day that the Spaniards have recaptured the island. His close friend Bart Kindness is a prisoner. Knowing the Spanish predilection for torture, Morgan resolves to rescue his friend. He gathers together the best captains in the Caribbean, missing only his friend Captain Mansfield. The ships first stop in Cuba for a small sacking expedition and gather "proof" of Spanish treachery and a plot to attack Jamaica. They proceed to Puerto Bello where, by the use of misleading tactics and clever strategy, Morgan takes the forts and recovers the ill-treated prisoners. Home again, he hears that the Spaniards have captured and hung Mansfield.

Using this as an excuse, he vows to fulfill the old man's dream and capture Maracaibo. Upon arrival at the Venezuelan city, Morgan finds the Spaniards have retreated before them, evacuating troops and treasure and leaving nothing. The Spanish navy entraps the men and the ships in the harbor. Only by feint and fire ship does Morgan make good an escape. Once again back in Jamaica, he learns that the Spaniards were responsible for the death of another dear friend. Gathering his ships, he prepares to attack Panama. The going is difficult, and plunder is small. Bart Kindness dies in the process and Morgan comes down with fever. Worse things are yet to come. Returning home, he discovers Modyford imprisoned and bound for London trial. In a year, he himself travels to London to be tried. Once there, he discovers that his ex-surgeon (the loathed and incompetent Exmeling) has written a wildly romanticized and damning tale of Morgan's adventures.

It was worse, far worse, than he had expected. There was no silliness too great for Exmeling to set down; no atrocity too hideous for Exmeling to invent. It was a monumental absurdity: a "pirate tale" such as seamen spin for illiterates over a tavern table in return for a drink; but it was also extremely readable, and it had a fascination of the frightful. One turned the page to find what new horror might be in store on the next. Little Henrik had found the perfect formula for selling a book.[4]

Morgan is incensed, as is Daviot. In time, Morgan is cleared by the government, whose relationships with Spain are again deteriorating and he sues Exmeling's publishers. Testimonials pour in refuting the absurd charges, and he is awarded damages. The king then appoints Morgan as Lieutenant Governor of Jamaica and knights him.

Of Daviot's non-mystery novels, *The Privateer* stands out as the most compelling and readable. Written in the best romantic traditions, this swashbuckling study of "Harry" Morgan, privateer and/or buccaneer, deserves to be reissued. Of all the works written under either the Daviot or Tey names, this one would most easily translate into film.

Published posthumously, *The Privateer* was well received. James Kelly in the *New York Times*,[5] terms it a "spanking good yarn." Edward Fitzgerald comments: "This last of her works is an action-packed adventure story in which she combines her interest in historical material with the sharp novelistic skill she demonstrated with her detective stories."[6]

Daviot captures the intensity and color of a turbulent era, drawing extremely fine distinctions between piracy and patriotism. Once again choosing an historic personage of tarnished reputation, she scrupulously polishes her hero into a gentleman. If not a scholar, Morgan is at least a clever, canny, inspiring leader. As Richard III was a much maligned, talented administrator, and Claverhouse a diplomatic, loyal rebel, so is the name of Henry Morgan cleared. Unlike *Claverhouse,* in which the reader and Dundee's personality are lost in the circumlocutions of Scottish history, *The Privateer* is more focused. Placed in the same period but centering in the Caribbean, the latter book concentrates more on the character of "Harry" Morgan and less on the history of Jamaica or the islands. Avoiding one of the problems of Claverhouse, Daviot does not attempt to describe Morgan's entire life. She concentrates instead on his progress from bondsman to privateer to knight. Of all her works, *The*

Privateer is undoubtedly the most dramatic and suspenseful. Concluding notes suggest both her approach to the subject and her personal concern in writing historical fiction.

To write fiction about historic fact is very nearly impermissible. It is permissible only on two conditions:
(a) That neither the inevitable simplication of plot nor the invention of detail shall be allowed to falsify the general picture;
(b) That the writer shall state where the facts may be found, so that the reader may, if he cares, compare the invention with the truth. (Author's Note to *The Privateer*)

In this final work, Daviot adds a surprising twist to her hero's character. Unlike Grant, Kif, Miss Pym, Brat Farrar, and all the others, Morgan is able to relate, communicate, and respond to individuals. He alone of all the Daviot/Tey characters has a believable, honest wife and devoted friends for whom he will put his life on the line. Doubtless the author's final painful and lonely year of life is reflected in this denial of isolation and withdrawal.

CHAPTER 4

The Man in the Queue

*T*HE *Man in the Queue*, Elizabeth Mackintosh's first mystery novel, was initially published in 1929 under the Daviot pseudonym. It received mixed reviews. P.E.R., the reviewer for the *Boston Transcript*, called the book "thoroughly well-written," insisting that it "goes beyond the demands usually made of this particular type of fiction."[1] Apparently, P.E.R. was not familiar with the contemporary demands of detective and mystery novels, since some of the greatest works in the genre were being written in this period. Among them were Philip Macdonald's *The White Crow* in 1928, Dashiel Hammet's *The Dain Curse* (1929) and *The Maltese Falcon* (1930), Margery Allingham's *Crime at Black Dudley*, Msgr. Ronald A. Knox's *The Footsteps at the Lock* (1928), *The Greene Murder Case* by S.S. Van Dine (1928), and Dorothy L. Sayers's *Clouds of Witness* and *The Unpleasantness at the Bellona Club* (both 1928). These novels rank among the most famous as well as the best written in the period. The reviewer for the *New York Times* suggests: "The story might have been rather better than the average detective yarn if the author had only refrained from revealing to us at great length the mental processes of the detective. Judicious pruning would have made the story much more readable."[2]

I *The "Rules"*

Considering both the competition and the vogue of the period, it is amazing that *The Man in the Queue* received any satisfactory reviews. Tradition during the early Golden Age of detective fiction demanded strict adherence to the "rules" laid down by various influential writers, among them S.S. Van Dine and Ronald A. Knox. Essentially, the rules insisted on a "puzzle novel," that is, one in which the reader as well as the detective is given a set number of suspects and clues and must, through logic, determine the criminal. The emphasis was on the how rather than the why of crime solving. Tey ignored a number of the rules. First, there is little if any actual detection. The solution to the crime is literally dumped in Grant's lap. Neither the reader nor the detective has an adequate chance to determine the murderer, since there are scarcely any clues pointing to her identity. The murderer, in fact, plays a very minor role in the novel as a whole. The means of murder is obvious and uncomplicated. Generally, in the Golden Age, devious and unusual methods of killing were used, the more unusual the better. Dorothy L. Sayers, for example, enjoyed creating new and different methods of murder for her novels. Van Dine insists that the solution to the problem "must at all times be obvious, providing the reader is clever enough to notice."[3] This is certainly not true of *Man in the Queue*, in which neither Grant nor the reader even suspect Mrs. Willis of being the murderer. Finally, Van Dine suggests the writer avoid long descriptive passages and character analyses, a matter Tey insisted upon.[4]

II   *The New Realism*

Slowly the obeisance to the rules began to diminish and by the beginning of World War II, the rules were regularly broken. After the war, the emphasis was focused more on the sociology of the crime—the motivations of the criminal and his environment. The authors became seriously concerned with the personalities of the detective and the criminal, concentrating on the why rather than how. Realism became the password, and the "hard-boiled dick" replaced the gentleman detective of the Golden Age. The "dick" was cruel, hard-drinking, fast-fisted, and prone to beatings and violence. Raymond Chandler in "The Simple Act of Murder" describes him as a complete man, a hero, honorable, poor, with a sense of character, lonely and proud, with a disgust for sham and pettiness.[5] The "dick" searches for hidden truth, is aware, sometimes witty, always common, and will take no man's insolence without taking a dispassionate revenge.

III   *Reevaluation*

When *The Man in the Queue* was republished in 1953, the reviews were enthusiastically favorable. The reasons are no doubt obvious. Tey spanned the bridge between the Golden Age and the era of the "hard boiled dick." Inspector Grant shared many of the same characteristics of both Peter Wimsey and Philip Marlowe. Like Wimsey, Grant was an independently wealthy gentleman with a fine palate and a "flair" for detection. Like Chandler's hero, Grant is instinctually honorable, with an excruciatingly keen conscience. Both are lonely and proud, with a contempt for pettiness and sham. Tey's emphasis on characterization and motivation rather than puzzling plot was the rule rather than the exception in the 1950s. She was, in fact, ahead of her time in 1929. Interestingly, *The Man in the Queue* was republished under the Tey pseudonym, thus setting aside her detective writings from her "serious novels," plays, and biography.

IV *The Plot*

The initial action in *The Man in the Queue* begins immediately after the murder has occurred. Tey also was to follow this formula in her next novel, *A Shilling for Candles* (1936), and in her last, *The Singing Sands* (1953). A group of people are crowding in a queue before a theater waiting to get tickets for one of the last performances of *Didn't You Know?*, a very popular play starring Ray Marcable, "that comet that two years ago had blazed out of the void into the zenith and had dimmed the known and constant stars." Her talented dancing and aloof smile had won the hearts of the public. Since she was leaving London to go on tour in America, her fans were particularly anxious to see her "one last time." Tey provides a striking picture of the English queue.

The queue twiddled its toes, and Cockneywise, made the most of whatever entertainment provided itself in the dark canyon of the lane. First there had come the newsboys, small things with thin, impassive faces and wary eyes. They had flickered down the queue like wildfire and disappeared, leaving behind a trail of chatter and fluttering papers. Then a man with legs shorter than his body laid a ragged strip of carpet on the damp pavement and proceeded to tie himself into knots until he looked as a spider does when it is taken unaware, his mournful toad's eye gleaming now and then from totally unexpected places . . .[6]

Street performers and venders plied the line until the ticket office opened and the crowd began to inch forward. As they push

forward, a fat woman protests, "Ere, I'll thank you to stop
shoving. Can't a lady be allowed to take out her purse without
everyone losing their manners?" (p.8) The man behind her,
however, did not respond. As she moves away, he sinks to the
ground. He is dead, a small dagger in his back. The fat woman
stares in horror, another woman screams, and a third moans to
her husband, "Oh, let's go home, Jimmy! Oh, let's go home!"
(p.9) Jimmy's wife sobs hysterically and the fat woman protests,
but the constable who arrives on the scene insists they remain to
be questioned.

Grant, the sophisticated, intelligent, courageous, dapper
Inspector, is assigned to the case. The facts are few. The man was
stabbed with a stiletto by a left-handed, strong man.

"Not a woman?"
"No, it would need more strength than a woman has to drive the blade
in as it has been driven. You see, there was no room for a backsweep of
the arm. The blow has to be delivered from a position of rest. Oh no, it
was a man's work. And a determined man's." (p.13)

This, of course, is the first error in assumption. By looking at the
man, Grant and the police surgeon determine that he is a "lost
cause" type (p. 13). "He had practical enough qualities in his
face, but his hands were a dreamer's"(p. 13). There is no
identification whatsoever on the body. As in *The Singing Sands*,
the identification of the victim occupies nearly as much space as
the tracking down of the murderer. Grant begins making a series
of assumptions based mostly on stereotype prejudices which lead
him completely astray.

No thorough Englishman used such a weapon. . . . the very femininity
of it proclaimed the Levant, or at the very least one used to Levantine
habits of life. A sailor perhaps. . . . The picturesqueness of the thing
was Levantine. (p. 16)

He continues speculating as to motive.

Revenge or jealousy? Most probably—Levantines were notoriously
vulnerable in their feelings; an insult rankled for a lifetime, a straying
smile on the part of their adored, and they ran amok. (p. 16)

Since the dead man was carrying a fully loaded revolver, Grant
assumes it is in some way directly involved with the death.

But then there was the unknown man's desire to slough his identity. A loaded revolver in these circumstances pointed to suicide. But if he contemplated suicide, why postpone it while he went to the play? What other motive induced a man to make himself anonymous? . . . Had he intended to shoot some one and, afraid of not getting away, made himself nameless? (p. 17)

Ironically, this is the answer to the puzzle, neatly sketched out in the second chapter. Grant, however, on the basis of his previous false assumptions, disregards the idea and follows a totally wrong path.

Grant interviews Mrs. James Ratcliffe, the hysterical woman, and five others who were in the queue but gets no new information. While interviewing the doorkeeper at the theater, Grant is invited to tea with Ray Marcable. He describes the stiletto to her and, to his surprise, there is a flash of recognition in her eyes. Later, of course, the reason for this becomes clear.

By the day of the inquest, Grant has no information to give the coroner. The corpse remains unidentified and Williams, Grant's faithful assistant, is given the man's tie in hope that a clerk might remember selling it. Again, the investigation comes up against a blank wall. The tie is a common one, sold all over England. The lab reports that the stiletto had a slight fracture in the handle which had cut the murderer's finger. "He would now be suffering from a jagged cut somewhere on the thumb side of the first finger on the left hand, or finger side of the thumb" (p. 30). Grant considers that the crime might have been a gang retribution against a backslider and interviews Danny Miller, a local gangster. Danny, immediately cleared because he is right-handed and has no cut on his finger, recognizes the man, but cannot identify him.

Grant's clues, thin indeed, are fortunately augmented by the arrival of a "plain, cheap, white envelope," addressed in "strong, plain capitals" (p. 37), and containing twenty five pounds "To bury the man who was found in the queue" (p. 37). As in *The Singing Sands*, the man's character is deduced from the handwriting: "Not well off. Not used to writing much. Clean. Smokes. Depressed" (p. 38).

Grant persuades Williams to dine with him at Laurent's, an exclusive restaurant where he was "a pet of the head waiter's" (p. 39). Interestingly, Tey does not go into detail concerning Grant's food or drink. In her later novels, *To Love and Be Wise*

and *The Singing Sands* in particular, the Inspector's sensitive
palate and delight in food and Scotch whiskey are much touted.
While they eat, Grant is aware that he is being watched from
behind the screen shielding the kitchen door. When Williams
accidentally-on-purpose knocks the screen over, however, no
one is there.

Back at the Yard, Grant identifies fingerprints from the letter
and the gun as being the same. Since they do not belong to the
dead man, he assumes that the friend who supplied the gun also
supplied the funeral money. Since the victim's fingerprints are
also on the notepaper, Grant with Holmesian logic deduces that
the "man who lent the gun and provided the money lived with
the dead man" (p. 42).

Late that night, a young man who identifies himself as working
at Laurent's arrives at Grant's home. He is Raoul Legarde, a
Frenchman, who was in the queue the night the man was killed.
He spoke briefly to the victim, and later noticed him talking
angrily with another man not belonging to the queue. He
describes the man and is prepared to identify him under oath.
Things, as Grant says, "were beginning to move" (p. 47). That
afternoon Danny Miller calls to tell Grant that he remembered
where he had seen the dead man.

"Well, I travelled in a race train to Leicester with him, end of January, I
think it was. . . . Sure? I remember as if it was yesterday. We talked
racing, and he seemed to know quite a lot about it. But I never saw
him before or since . . . Eh? . . . No, I didn't see any bookmaking
things. . . ." (p. 56)

On Monday, Grant learns from a bank manager that the notes
sent for the funeral were part of a withdrawal of two hundred
and twenty-three pounds ten shillings—from the account of
Albert Sorrell, small local bookmaker. The cashier describes
Sorrell and there is no question that he is the dead man.
However, the money was withdrawn by a dark, thin man of
medium height with high cheekbones. "Foreign-looking, a little"
(p. 72). Undoubtedly it was Grant's "Levantine." Grant is
delighted at the possibilities opened by this disclosure—
blackmail, for example, always a very nice motive.

Quickly the Inspector goes to Sorrell's office. The rooms are
totally devoid of clues. His next call is on Laury Murray, one of

the biggest bookmakers in London. Murray takes him to the track and introduces him to Sorrell's business associates. Tey, a devoted follower of the races, was apparently acquainted well enough with bookies to describe them and their business practices accurately and intimately in two novels. In *The Man in the Queue* the victim is of course a bookie. In *Kif,* published in 1929, the same year as *The Man in the Queue,* the main character for a time is employed as a bookie. At the track, Grant is able only to ascertain Sorrell's address; no one knew anything of his companions. The Inspector quickly interviews Mrs. Everett, Bert Sorrell's landlady. "A bony, shortsighted woman" (p. 85), she insists that Sorrell was planning to leave for America. He had shared his rooms with Jerry Lamont whose picture identifies him as "the Levantine." Mrs. Everett nervously denies any knowledge of Lamont's whereabouts. Grant suspects she is not being "straight" with him.

On his way home after dinner, Grant suddenly recognizes the "Levantine," as he chooses to call the man described by Raoul. He chases the man through the London streets but is unable to catch him. The Inspector consoles himself with the knowledge that the man is still in London. "But Grant knew the Londoner's mulish habit of clinging to the town he knows, and the foreigner's ratlike preference of the sewers to the open" (p. 61). Grant, and also Tey, the reader might assume, was not fond of foreigners. This dislike and distrust is typical of the Golden Age of detective fiction. Agatha Christie's Hercule Poirot, for example, is often considered odd and perhaps even unreliable since he is a foreigner. Even Dorothy L. Sayers had a latent distrust of foreigners and Jews as seen in *Whose Body?*

Stimulated by the chase, Grant drops in to see Ray Marcable perform. Here Tey's interesting attitude toward actors and particularly actresses is expressed. Marcable, smiling sweetly, continually upstages her leading man. There is a certain calculated cruelty about her actions that shocks Grant.

She *was* keeping the man out of it. When he looked for the indications they were all there, but they were done with a subtlety such as Grant had never witnessed before. There was nothing so crude as trying to share or divert his applause, or even cutting his applause short by an intrusion of her own. . . . (p. 65)

Instead, she uses her "glowing personality with unscrupulous-
ness" (p. 65). Tey's actresses are uniformly self-centered, often
remote, and usually always charming. Marta Hallard in Tey's
later novels occasionally manages a small smattering of sensitivity and insight as far as Grant is concerned.

After Grant leaves, Mrs. Everett quickly puts some food in a
basket and, taking precautions against being followed, goes to
see Lamont. She tells him

"I came because there was no time to write to you, and I had to see you.
They've found out who he was. A man from Scotland Yard came this
evening, and wanted to know all about you both. . . . But he knows
you are in London, and it's only a matter of time if you stay here. You've
got to go." (pp. 93–94)

He must either escape or give himself up, she insists. " 'Bert was
right when he christened you Lady Macbeth,' he said". (p. 95)
She plans his escape to her family home in Scotland. She will
accompany him part way to allay any suspicions, pretending he is
her son. Her plan works out perfectly.

Grant meanwhile discovers that Sorrell was in fact booked to
America on the *Queen Arabia* and so, surprisingly, was Mrs.
James Ratcliffe, the sobbing, hysterical woman from the queue.
Interviewing Ratcliffe again, Grant discovers that the woman,
Margaret, was going to visit her sister in New York. Grant sends
detectives disguised as peddlers to Ratcliffe's to discover all they
can about the couple's home life. They learn little, aside from the
fact that Mrs. Ratcliffe tends to have a wicked temper, mostly
employed against her husband.

Williams discovers Lamont's hiding place, but of course, the
suspect has escaped to Scotland. Grant, investigating Mrs.
Everett and discovering that she was from Scotland and was seen
with a young man at King's Cross station, resolves to go to
Inverness at once.

Grant, delighted to be again in the Highlands, travels from
Inverness to Carninnish, the home of Mrs. Everett's family.
Arranging both to indulge in his favorite sport and watch for
Lamont, Grant fishes in the river and waits. Lamont is staying at
the manse with the minister, Mrs. Dinmont, the minister's sister,
and Miss Dinmont, his niece. That evening, the minister, Mr.
Logan, noticing Grant fishing, providentially invites him in for

tea. Lamont recognizes him at once, but makes no immediate overt move. After tea, the Inspector casually invites "Mr. Lowe" to join him in a brief walk. Lamont goes with him, but once outside the house tosses pepper in Grant's eyes and runs away. Again Grant must chase his quarry, this time through the rocks and hills of Carninnish. Lamont steals a rowboat and heads downstream. Grant, however, quickly borrows a motorboat and follows. As they approached Lamont's boat,

. . . Lamont, coatless and hatless, sprang to his feet and then to the gunnel, as if to dive. His stockinged foot slipped on the wet gunnel, his feet went from under him. With a sickening crack that they heard quite distinctly, the back of his head hit the boat and he disappeared under water. (p. 154)

Grant dives in and rescues the injured suspect, and carries him back to a nearby house. Miss Dinmont quickly arrives to nurse the ill man. She is the first of Tey's intelligent, down-to-earth, realistic ingenues. Neither as clever nor witty as Erica in *A Shilling for Candles*, she nonetheless exhibits the same loyalty toward the suspect, refusing to believe his guilt.

It is her doubt, as it is Erica's doubt, that sparks Grant's conscience. The evidence, including a scar on Lamont's finger, is circumstantial, but damning. Lamont tells Grant his story. Bert was planning to leave for America but didn't want Lamont to see him off. As a sort of going away bash, they went to see the matinee of *Didn't You Know?* After the show, they parted and Lamont returned to his new rooms. Before saying goodbye, however, "he gave me a little packet and said I was to promise not to open it till the day after tomorrow—that was the day after he sailed" (p. 171).

While he was unpacking in his new rooms, Lamont realized his revolver was missing. "And then I grew frightened somehow . . . I began to remember how quiet Bert had been lately" (p. 172). He went quickly back to the theater and found Bert in the queue. He admitted taking the revolver and insisted it was in his luggage. "I began to feel small and to feel I'd made a fool of myself. . . . So I told him to keep his ticket and the revolver too, and went away" (p. 173). On Thursday when he opened the parcel, he discovered all of Bert's cash. It was then that he discovered that Bert was the man in the queue. Knowing they

were seen arguing and now having Bert's money, Lamont knew
he was in a difficult position and so went to Mrs. Everett. She
helped him, hid him, and eventually aided his escape.

Questioned about Sorrell's personal life, Lamont insists that his
friend told him nothing. Occasionally he received letters in a
feminine handwriting, but he would never talk about them.

Grant begins torturing himself with doubts and is uneasy about
the arrest. "Is this an example of the famous flair?" (p. 183) asks
his chief. With his usual terrier-like persistence, Grant goes to
Waterloo station to examine Sorrell's luggage. He finds a small
brooch formed in an intricate monogram "M.R.," but cannot
locate any connection between the jewelry and Margaret
Ratcliffe. He persuades Miss Dinmont to act as his cousin and
trap Mrs. Ratcliffe into admitting she recognized the brooch.
This too does not work. Grant's temper deteriorates markedly.
His "other self" argues with him incessantly, convinced that the
circumstantial evidence is insufficient. In Tey's novels, the
"other self" argues with her protagonists, and without exception,
wins the argument. Lucy Pym agrees to keep her knowledge of
the crime secret in *Miss Pym Disposes*. Brat Farrar agrees to
become a criminal in *Brat Farrar*. And Grant's other self insists
always that he stay on a case that seems either solved or at a
dead end.

When the Inspector is finally determined to give up, "to
believe what I see and know, and not what I feel" (p. 209), Mrs.
Wallis, the fat woman from the queue appears in his office. She
says, "I came because I think this business has gone far enough. I
killed Bert Sorrell, and I'm not going to let any one suffer for it if
I can 'elp it" (p. 210). The incredulous Grant listens to her story.
She killed him because he was going to shoot "my Rosie," that is
her daughter, Rosie Markham whose stage name was Ray
Marcable. Rosie and Bert had gone together before she became
famous. Once she was a star, however, Ray Marcable wanted
nothing to do with a small time bookie. The brooch had been
made for the actress. Sorrell was going to murder the girl and
then kill himself.

The doctors pronounced Mrs. Wallis quite sane and fit to plead, and her
trial is due at the Old Bailey this month. Grant is convinced that he will
get off, and I am inclined to trust Grant's flair so far. Unwritten laws, he
says, are not supposed to be valid in this country, but a British jury is in

reality just as sentimental as a French one; and when they hear the story as put forward by Mrs. Wallis's counsel. . . . they'll weep bucketfuls and refuse to convict her. (p. 223)

The Man in the Queue contains some of the weaknesses expected in a first novel. Since this was Tey's first experiment in detective fiction, this is not surprising. Yet *Kif,* published the same year, is a tightly written, brilliantly composed novel, with none of the flaws seen in *The Man in the Queue.* One might suspect that Tey patterned the structure of her first detective novel after those by Freeman Wills Crofts, well known for his detailed descriptions of endless police procedures. This would explain the unnecessary but involved passages dealing with the identification of Lamont's tie, for example, as well as the long explication of Ray Marcable's character. In addition, the lack of sufficient foreshadowing creates an unsatisfactory and unbelievable conclusion. Mrs. Wallis's confession is too convenient to be artistic. In fact, it is the coincidences that hold the novel together. For example, that a kitchen worker at Grant's favorite restaurant should also have been standing behind the murdered man in the queue could perhaps be accepted were it not for the coincidences that follow. Lamont is seen by Grant walking down the same street. Mrs. Ratcliffe, who just happened to be in the queue, also just happened to be booked to travel to America on Sorrell's ship. The brooch, with the initials RM, was so conveniently misread as MR and assumed to belong to Mrs. Ratcliffe.

V   *Tey's Conventions*

Aside from the coincidences and Grant's erroneous assumptions, the basic plot of the novel closely resembles Tey's second detective novel, *A Shilling for Candles.* The corpse is initially unidentified, as in *The Singing Sands.* Grant searches for and obtains the identity of the victim. In most of Tey's novels, the victims are "not as good as they could be." Only in *The Daughter of Time,* where the victims are the innocent nephews of Richard III, and in *The Singing Sands* where the victim is a naive pilot, does Tey deal with likable individuals. In *A Shilling for Candles,* Grant again assumes an innocent is guilty of the crime. This is true of every Inspector Grant novel with the exception of *The*

Singing Sands. Grant chases the suspect into hiding where he becomes ill. Grant then insists on the suspect's innocence, and ultimately the true criminal is brought to justice. Grant does some detection, but most of his discoveries are either accidental or coincidental.

VI   *Grant's Character*

In *Man in the Queue,* Tey describes Grant physically for the first and only time.

If Grant had an asset beyond the usual ones of devotion to duty and a good supply of brains and courage, it was that the last thing he looked like was a police officer. He was of medium height and slight in build, and he was—now, if I say dapper, of course you will immediately think of something like a tailor's dummy . . . and Grant is most certainly not that; but if you can visualize a dapperness that is not of the tailor's dummy type, then that is Grant. (p. 11)

Throughout the novels, Grant is proud of his "flair," though his superiors continually warn him to keep it in check. Perhaps the most realistic aspect of his character is his ambivalence. Sensitive to the point of occasional agony, he nonetheless is more than willing to accept stereotypes. For example, he refers to "the foreigner's ratlike preference of the sewers to the open" (p. 61). And later, "Typically French he was, he thought, in his shrewd recognition of the commercial worth of his beauty, in his humour, in his opportunism" (p. 91). Grant, like Tey's other protagonists, indulges in orgies of self-blame and endless arguments with his "other self." It is no wonder that in *The Singing Sands,* he is rapidly approaching a nervous breakdown.

Finally, Tey creates the imperfect detective. His logic, deductions, conclusions, are inevitably slightly wrong. Yet, he is not a comical figure, demanding more pity than laughter since he wholeheartedly believes in the rightness of his actions before and during, and wholeheartedly doubts them afterward. Throughout the novels, it is clear that the Inspector loves his work. Tey points out that his independent income could mean easy retirement, but apparently his Puritan conscience insists on work. Generally, he himself does most of the interviewing and research. It is only in *The Man in the Queue* that he has detectives adopt disguises to obtain information.

VII   *The Women*

In *The Man in the Queue* Tey introduces some "stock characters" which, with minor variation, appear in many of her novels. Ray Marcable, for example, is a talented, sophisticated, self-centered actress, a bit hard, perhaps, but successful. Renamed Marta Hallard, this character type reappears in most Inspector Grant novels. Miss Dinmont, the clever, intuitive young woman, becomes in later novels Tey's beloved ingenue whose character judgments can always be relied upon. The ingenue is independent, sensitive, witty, and inevitably champions some doubtful young man. With the exception of Ruth in *Brat Farrar* who champions Simon, the murderer, the ingenue is always right.

Mrs. Everett and Grant's housekeeper Mrs. Field are doubles. Both are concerned with the well-being of the men they care for. Both are equally certain that their man is correct in all matters, with the exception of his health. Here he needs constant reminders, attention, and care so that he does not neglect his stomach nor his sleep. Both worry constantly, fuss continually and see their duty in life revolving around protecting and feeding their charge. In later novels, this character type becomes a kindly aunt, a fussy spinster, or an intuitive cousin. Mrs. Wallis too fits this type. She acts murderously, it is true, to save her daughter and her daughter's reputation. She is, in fact, aside from Beau Nash in *Miss Pym Disposes*, Tey's only murderer who does not act from jealousy and self-interest.

VIII   *The Youthful Suspect*

Lamont is a foolish and weak young man, a type which appears in Tey's earlier novels and then again in *To Love and Be Wise*. Insecure, frightened, unstable and unwise, Lamont acts from emotion, not thought. Like Tisdall in *A Shilling for Candles*, his first and most immediate concern is for himself. And like Walter in *To Love and Be Wise*, he is a victim both of police suspicion as well as his own foolish actions. The immature young man in Tey's novels is generally selfish and often boring but, nonetheless, he wins the affection of a wise and understanding ingenue who defends him, feeds him, and cares for him as a mother would for a clumsy and perhaps none too bright child.

IX *Symbolism*

Throughout her works, Tey uses a carefully interwoven set of symbols which reflect both her own personal opinions as well as the theme of the novel. In *The Man in the Queue*, the two most apparent symbols at once obvious are the queue and the stiletto. The queue suggests both patience as well as an impatience for what one desires. Standing in line for several hours, the people amuse themselves and are amused easily. But when the box office opens, there is a shuffling, a pushing, an irritation similar to that which Grant experiences in his hunt for the murderer. The dagger or stiletto is, of course, a masculine symbol. Sharp and cutting, it injures both the victim and the murderer. Grant and the police surgeon immediately identify it as a weapon used by a man, and Grant assumes a "Levantine" since an Englishman would use his fists, a razor, a bludgeon, or, as a last resort, a gun. But never, Grant insists, would a true Englishman use a stiletto. Ironically, the dagger was used by Ray Marcable when she played Lady Macbeth in a high school play. Later, it was used by her mother, again in a Lady Macbeth fashion to destroy someone who threatened the happiness, wealth, and health of her beloved daughter. The dagger is the only symbol that does not involve emotion. Mrs. Wallis used it, one might assume, as the housewife would use a pesticide, to rid the environment of a noisome, dangerous insect.

The brooch, on the other hand, is a female symbol of beauty and pride. Equally misinterpreted as the dagger, it points Grant in the completely wrong direction. Sorrell sent the brooch to Ray Marcable, and she returned it with distaste and irritation. He in turn was deeply angered and secretly vowed revenge.

Of all possible symbols, Tey's most repeated are those of the journey and the river or pond. Grant inevitably must journey somewhere to obtain clues, information or leads; his journeys become kinds of quests both for information on the crime and for facts about the individuals involved. In Tey's first novel, Grant journeys to Scotland in search of a criminal. In her last novel, *The Singing Sands*, he journeys to Scotland in search of himself and in the process discovers both a crime and a criminal. The quest is never easy and always involves some agonizing for the detective. Nonetheless, it aids him finally in reaching a correct and logical conclusion.

Tey, always enamored of the countryside, obviously enjoyed fishing as well as the beauties of rivers and streams. In *The Man in the Queue,* Grant journeys briefly upon a river and ends up rescuing the suspect from certain death by drowning. His immersion, so to speak, foreshadows a rebirth of attitude in which he begins to suspect that Lamont is not guilty of the crime. In *The Singing Sands,* Grant becomes renewed, reinvigorated, and rejuvenated by his trip to Cladda and walk to the sea. In *To Love and Be Wise,* the river is dragged for the missing body, but yields up nothing but an old shoe. Grant's doubt about the victim's death is given rebirth in the process and propels him back to London to discover the truth about Leslie and Lee Searle.

X   *Police and the Common Man*

Tey's opinion of Scotland Yard and the police force is not as flattering in *The Man in the Queue* as it might be. The police, it seems, are inadequate, and though well meaning, they often apprehend the wrong man. And, she continues, they just as often are willing to settle for the apparent solution of a case rather than the truth. As Raoul Legard states, "I do not trust the Sureté. They make very much out of nothing" (p. 46). Tey's opinion of the general public is equally unflattering. They are foolish, for example, in the way they dote on obviously self-centered, egotistic actresses. They are willing to be lined up for hours, to be pushed and shoved, to stand crushed like sardines to see a famous person perform. Juries made up of the average Britisher are perhaps inadequate, definitely stupid. "Grant surveyed them sardonically, and thanked the gods that neither his case nor his life depended on their intelligences" (p. 34).

XI   *Themes*

Since there is no wicked, unrepentant criminal in *The Man in the Queue* (a rarity in Tey's novels), she does not indulge in her usual attacks against the depravity and vanity of the criminal and the laxity of the penal system. She does, however, in this first novel, reiterate on a minor note the hells of war. "To go out into the street tonight would be like walking into no-man's land with Fritz machine-gunning" (p. 95), states Lamont, for example. Her belief in heredity which is enlarged upon in *The Franchise Affair* is briefly stated here. "His grandmother had been Italian, and if he hadn't inherited the knife he probably inherited the will to use one . . ." (p. 206). Finally, the most pervading theme in all of Tey's novels is that of deception. Appearances to the author were almost always deceiving. A man who appeared guilty was in fact innocent while a kindly fat old woman was in fact a murderer. Individuals making a big show of their Christianity like Mrs. Everett, for example, were not above ignoring the law or using it to their own advantage if need be. A popular, sweet-smiling actress, is in fact an egotistic, cruel monster. This theme of disillusionment occurs in all Tey's fiction with the exception of her last, non-detective novel, *The Privateer*.

CHAPTER 5

A Shilling for Candles

A Shilling for Candles could aptly be called a successful rewrite of Tey's first novel, *The Man in the Queue.* The plot is similar, though more elaborately embellished with subplots, and the characters are more realistic. Again an innocent person is suspected of the crime and hounded into illness by Inspector Grant before he discovers his error. And like Lamont in *The Man in the Queue,* Tisdall, the accused but innocent character, ultimately escapes punishment. Again the identity of the corpse is not immediately known. Then too, the characters are in some way involved with the theater. There is also some mystery about the life of the victim as well as that of the suspect. Again a kindly, sharp-witted woman aids the suspect in eluding the police. There is, however, much more foreshadowing, clues, red herrings and the like—in short, more of the paraphernalia of a detective novel. And finally, the climax is more gripping, and there is far more preparation for the denouement.

I *The Plot*

The novel begins with what Scott Sutherland in *Blood in Their Ink* calls the method of sudden plunge.[1] The body of a girl is discovered on a beach by the English Channel. Although she is wearing a bright green expensive swim suit and is very attractive, no one is able to identify the girl or answer the usual questions. Where did she come from? How did she get there? Where are her clothes? The only clue is an ankle bracelet with each link shaped like a "C". Suddenly a man dashes down to the beach.

He stumbled into their compact circle without looking at them pushing aside the two policemen who had unconsciously interposed their bulk between him and the body.

61

"Oh, yes, it is!" he cried, and without warning sat down and burst into loud tears.[2]

The constable attempts to comfort him and at the same time, discover something about the dead girl. However, while the man admits "She's my hostess" (p. 13), he claims to be unaware of her name although he had stayed with her for five days. He called her Chris, and he is Robert Stannaway Tisdall; he admits to stealing her car, but cannot explain his actions. At Chris's cottage, the cook, Mrs. Pitts, identifies the girl as Chris Robinson from London. The house was rented from Owen Hughes who is "doing a film in Hollywood" (p. 13). Abruptly, a man flings open the door and shouts for Chris. He is Jay Harmer, songwriter, and identifies the girl as Christine Clay, famous movie star. The public is delighted with the sensation but,

It might have been observed by any student of nature not too actively engaged in the consequences of it that Christine Clay's death, while it gave rise to pity, dismay, horror, regret, and half a dozen other emotions in varying degrees, yet seemed to move no one to grief. The only outburst of real feeling had been that hysterical crisis of Robert Tisdall over her body. (p. 27)

As in the following novel, *Miss Pym Disposes*, the victim is acceptable but not lovable. It is possible that Tisdall's emotion was after all only self-pity. In fact, "Lydia Keats was openly jubilant" (p. 28); she had prophesied the death and was delighting in her sensation. Her larger-than-life ego makes her suspect, to the reader if not to the police.

In chapter 4, Tey introduces "Jammy" Hopkins, a character who reoccurs occasionally in several other of the author's novels. A journalist with "an excellent nose for jam" (p. 29) or news, Hopkins is intrigued to see Inspector Grant at the inquest.

Tey in both *The Man in the Queue* and *A Shilling for Candles* often changes point of view. The inquest, for example, is viewed from Jammy's sharp and observant eyes and an entirely different voice emerges than that of either Grant or the sometimes intrusive narrator. Tey's ability to differentiate so clearly the dialogue patterns allows her to create distinct and memorable characters.

Discovering that the inquest is to be adjourned, Jammy assumes the death was murder, and quickly tries to befriend

Tisdall. Grant, however, intervenes. Tisdall's irrational and hysteric reaction is similar to Lamont's in *The Man in the Queue*. Instead of bolting, however: "His face was like parchment, dry and old and expressionless. Only the pulse beating hard at his temple suggested a living being . . . And then, seeing a man's knees beginning to sag, Grant took him hastily by the arm" (p. 32–33). With the help of some brandy, Tisdall recovers sufficiently to explain himself. He had inherited a good deal of money, but like a "perfect fool" (p. 36), he'd spent every penny when Chris picked him up. Once again, Grant takes a liking to the suspect, and typically tries to deny his feelings. "Charm. The most insidious weapon in all the human armoury. And here it was being exploited under his nose" (p. 40).

He queries Tisdall about an overcoat. Tisdall claims, "It was stolen from the car one day when we were over at Dymchurch" (p. 41). Brusquely, Grant reveals that a button, apparently from an overcoat, had been found tangled in the victim's hair. At this point Erica, the chief constable's daughter, enters and Tisdall faints. The girl immediately takes over and revives Tisdall. She is, it quickly appears, a precocious, amusing "child" of seventeen with more character sense than Grant. Like Desterro in *Miss Pym Disposes*, Erica is the outspoken, intuitive judge of character and action.

"Well, what did he faint for? Is he guilty?"
"I don't know," Grant said, before he thought.
"I shouldn't think so." She was considering the now spluttering Tisdall. "He doesn't look capable of much." This with the same grave detachment as she used to everything she did. (p. 45)

Grant, deciding to dismiss his suspect temporarily, suggests he get a job. Providentially, a waiter at a nearby resort hotel was stabbed and his job is available.

There is no longer any question of murder, both because of the evidence of the button and because Clay's nails were broken from clawing at something. Grant discusses the crime with Sergeant Williams who, in the early chapters, serves as a Watson. Instead of agonizing and analyzing inwardly, Grant's information and deductions, if not his emotions, are presented in dialogue form. Williams assumes Tisdall is guilty and provides rational explanations for all his irrational actions. Grant, ever the neat detective, would like a motive. This, of course, is "granted" him

shortly. The detective sergeant, like Peter Wimsey's Bunter, is a
source of interesting and sometimes essential information. He
reveals that the actress was born in Nottingham. Each fan
magazine, however, was given a different version of her life.
Clay was obviously unsure of her own identity, suiting the story
to fit her moods. "No one ever knew where they were with
her. . . . People can only get at you if they know what you're
like . . . If you keep them guessing, they're the victims, not you"
(p. 53). Insisting that Clay was "vulnerable," Williams suggests
that Harmer had a motive and no alibi. Grant dismisses this idea.
He does decide to get further information about Clay and visits
Marta Hallard, a leading actress who will appear significantly in
The Daughter of Time, Tey's most famous novel.

Clay, married to Lord Edward Champneis, apparently had no
lovers, yet was not well liked by other women. Judy Sellers, "a
sulky fair girl who played 'dumb' blondes" (p. 53) insists that
Harmer is guilty. Everyone joins in to guess the guilty person.
Only Chris's husband is not suspect since he was out of England
until the day after her death.

Having obtained little significant information about the
victim's habits and friends, Grant pursues the source of the
button. He continues to hope that Tisdall's coat with missing
button, will be found. He has further discovered that Harmer
spent the night before the murder sleeping in his car, but has no
one to corroborate his story.

Grant then meets with Edward Champneis and Erskine, Clay's
lawyer. Her will is fairly direct: no money to her wealthy
husband, a few legacies, with the bulk of her fortune "for the
preservation of the beauty of England" (p. 84). The last legacy
read "To my brother Herbert, a shilling for candles" (p. 84).
This, Grant states, "is the first sign of real enmity I have
discovered among Miss Clay's relationships. One never knows
what it might lead us to" (p. 85). A codicil written the day before
her death leaves her California ranch plus five thousand pounds
to Tisdall. Here then is Grant's motive.

The detective and the bereaved husband stop at a pub,
commenting meanwhile on the disappointing vulgarity of people
in general. Champneis speaks of Galeria, a country he recently
visited which "mislaid their spectacular patriot" (p. 88), Rimmik.
This foreshadows the revelation of Champneis' involvement in
Galerian politics. Following stage tradition, what appear to be

insignificant comments or actions prove later essential to plot evolvement.

The inevitable warrant is issued for Tisdall, and Grant goes to the hotel to make the arrest. In Tisdall's room, Grant assumes "there was going to be no trouble" (p. 95). Again his assumption is wrong. Tisdall locks himself in a cupboard and Grant shouts "Poison is a fool's trick. We'll get you soon enough to give you an antidote . . ." (p. 97). He discovers too late that the cupboard is in fact a fire stairway and that Tisdall has escaped.

Back at his temporary office, Grant is plagued with useless "sightings" of the suspect. Unlike Freeman Wills Crofts, who would carefully detail each dead-end lead, Tey briskly sums up: "By Tuesday noon Tisdall had been seen in almost every corner of England and Wales, and by tea-time was beginning to be seen in Scotland" (p. 101).

In chapter 10, Tey introduces a very subtle joke. Williams comments, "It might be worse . . . so far no nut has come to confess to the crime, and waste our time that way. But the nut arrived next morning" (p. 102).

The "nut" is Judy Sellers. Since she knows nothing of the way Clay was drowned, her innocence is obvious. However, she does insist that Tisdall could not have committed the crime.

While the police are unable to locate their suspect, Erica is much more successful. She locates Tisdall hiding alongside the road and offers to help him. Like Mrs. Everett in *The Man in the Queue*, she does not believe the accused is guilty and aids and protects him. Both women offer food and are frank and straightforward with the "criminals" but not with the police. Erica, however, unlike Mrs. Everett, attempts to find the missing coat and prove Tisdall innocent. She is also compassionate and sensitive, more like Miss Dinmont in that respect than the cold Mrs. Everett.

Tisdall describes his coat to Erica—a small burn hole on the right side makes it unique. Since Tisdall refuses to surrender, Erica is determined to see that he is fed and freed of the accusation.

Persuading the head groom to lend her money for gas, Erica sets out to locate the missing coat. First, however, she returns to the place Tisdall was last seen and leaves him food, candy, and cigarettes, accurately assuming ". . . no 'local' had stolen that coat. She had lived all her life in a country community and knew very well that a new black overcoat cannot make its appearance even on the meanest back without receiving a truly remarkable amount of attention" (p. 124). She searches for a "casual" or tramp. Her first stop, at a trucker's café for a meal, informs her that "Harrogate Harry," a china mender known to steal coats and boots, was in the area. After a great deal of searching, Erica locates Harry. Determined and desperate, she asks "What did you do with the coat you took at Dymchurch?" (p. 135) She offers money, saying imaginatively

"It's to get Hart out of trouble . . . He shouldn't have left the car unattended. The owner is coming back tomorrow and if the coat isn't found by then Hart will lose his job."
    "Who's 'Art?" asked a woman. "Your brother?"
    "No. Our chauffeur". (p. 136)

Later Erica adds, to make it seem convincing, " 'I'm desperately in love with him,' Erica said, in the tone in which one says: 'And a box of matches, please.' At school theatricals Erica had always had charge of the curtains" (p. 137). Harry finally admits selling the coat to a stonebreaker and, for a pound note, remembers the address.

    Later that evening, Erica invites Grant to dinner. Her father, hoping to cheer the detective, encourages him to relax. Grant, echoing the words of Miss Pym, states "As a detective I'm a grand farmer" (p. 141). At dinner, talk inevitably turns to the missing Tisdall. The other dinner guest, a "nerve specialist," comments "You were surprised in your heart of hearts that he had done it. Perhaps even sorry. You hadn't believed it" (p. 141). Others, it seems, know Grant better than he does himself.

    The nerve specialist adds to one of the subplots by stating that he had travelled up from Dover with Champneis on Thursday. Champneis had not come over on the boat from Calais, but had used his yacht. For some reason, then, he had misled the police.

    Erica presents Tisdall's coat and Grant, angry and exhausted, realizes he must begin again. Here is a small flaw in the author's reasoning. On the basis of Clay's cook's identification of the coat, Grant assumes the man is innocent. The assumption, while correct, is illogical. Surely Tisdall could have obtained another coat, stolen it, perhaps, with the thought of murder in mind.

Nonetheless, Grant now assumes either Harmer or Champneis must be guilty, although he also begins tracking Clay's missing brother. Tisdall, meanwhile, cannot be located.

Tey at this point reveals the sensitivity that accounts for a large part of her present popularity.

He noticed with his usual self-awareness that he had no intention of going to Champneis and asking for an account of his movements on Wednesday night. It would be highly embarrassing, for one thing, if Champneis proved that he had slept peacefully in his bunk all night. Or at the Lord Warden. Or otherwise had a perfect alibi. For another—oh well, there was no getting away from the fact; one didn't demand information from the son of a ducal house as one demanded it from a coster. A rotten world, no doubt, but one must conform. (p. 152)

Inwardly chafing at the "double standard," Grant discovers that Champneis left the yacht Wednesday night as soon as it landed.

Grant continues to receive information about Chris's life and her brother, Herbert, who was "A nasty piece of work . . . As slimy, sneaking, cadging, self-satisfied a piece of human trash as you'd meet in a month of Sundays" (p. 95). He had taken up religion as an easy, fast way to swindle the unwary. In this novel, unlike *The Man in the Queue,* Tey introduces a subplot and an important character late in the work. Herbert, the ne'er-do-well brother, is as colorful, unique, and well portrayed as Erica, if not as appealing. In order to trap the missing brother, Grant persuades Erskine, the lawyer, to advertise that "if Herbert Gotobed will call at . . . [the] office he will hear of something to his advantage" (p. 199).

Here then Grant is stymied. As in *The Man in the Queue,* the leads are fruitless. Instead of suspense, Tey creates a mood of depression and futility. No approach seems to work for the detective, and the press, headed by Jammy, are demanding that the innocent "victim" Tisdall be located.

Jammy, irritated by the snappish attitude of Scotland Yard, attends a lecture on astrology by Lydia Keats. The audience is packed with "smart society," ". . . those longshoed, long-nosed, long-pedigreed people who lived on their places and not on their wits" (p. 183). Jammy watches the audience, assuming the murderer to be present, as indeed she is. Marta Hallard, "brittle, insincere sophisticate" (p. 187), is in the audience also. (The author's attitude toward Marta changes considerably in the later novels.

Marta is staring at Jay Harmer, and Jammy, like so many Tey characters, jumps to the assumption that the actress loves the songwriter. With the exception of the ingenue character, all of Tey's major characters are prone to quick and false assumptions. In detective and mystery novel theory this builds up suspense, though the technique is found more frequently in the "hard-boiled dick" novels of Hammett and Chandler than in the Golden Age writings of Sayers, for example.

During the question and answer period, Lydia announces "And one thing I have known ever since I stepped on the platform. The murderer of Christine Clay is here in this hall" (p. 193). The panic caused by her statement clears the hall.

On Wednesday afternoon, Grant goes to an accommodation address in Canterbury and waits for Herbert to collect Erskine's letter. A man in monk's garb appears and, noticing Grant, turns and abruptly disappears into the night. There is a pseudomonastery around the corner and Grant immediately calls on the director. The Reverend Father denies the presence of Herbert, but allows Grant to attend a service and look at the faces of the community. Surprisingly the altar and accessories are quite elaborate and expensive. Grant notices "A round sallow face on a round ill-shaped head, the eyes small, the nose fleshy, the lower lip loose, so that it hung away from his teeth as he repeated the words of the service" (p. 210). This monk's peculiar walk confirms his identity as Herbert. In the monastery he is called Brother Aloysius and will be put in charge of the entire operation in a month. He denies any knowledge of Herbert. Grant follows Brother Aloysius to a nearby house. The escape is the equivalent to Lamont's flight in *The Man in a Queue*. Suddenly, again as in the previous novel, Grant is attacked and the suspect escapes. The detective confiscates several false passports from the house.

Grant now makes a number of rapid discoveries. First, The Holy Order of the Tree of Lebanon is said to have a lot of money laid away. Since Herbert nearly had his hands on it, he has no motive for his sister's murder. Second, Harmer had met Champneis's yacht and gone off with him somewhere in a motorboat. Third, it occurs to Grant that murdering Clay from a motorboat would be the best and most convenient method.

Finally, in the early hours, Tisdall bursts into Grant's room, ecstatic that he is no longer suspect. He has been hiding in the attic of the hotel and stealing food from the kitchen. He is, however, quite ill and near pneumonia from his exposure in a thunderstorm.

With sudden inspiration, Grant deduces the motive for Champneis's and Harmer's actions and while reading a movie magazine gets another inspiration. He asks for a boat and, at 276 River Walk, he and Williams break into a boat cabin and discover the coat with the missing button. At the house they arrest Lydia Keats for the murder.

Lydia Keats had made three startling prophecies.

Her third statement prophesied the death by drowning of a woman start of the first magnitude whose name, of course, she gave, but the sob sister equally, of course, could not reveal. "If this third prophecy, so circumstantial, so unequivocal, comes true, then Miss Keats is established as the possessor of one of the most uncanny talents in the world. All humanity will be besieging her. But don't go swimming with Miss Keats, little blonde star! The temptation might be too much for her! (p. 248)

II   Inspector Grant

Inspector Grant in A *Shilling for Candles* seems both more at ease, sure of himself, and more realistic. Nonetheless, his doubts about his own judgment still occur, though he often attempts to deny them.

And for a moment doubt stirred in Grant. That had been beautifully done. Timing, expression, action. No professional actor could have done it better. But the doubt passed. He recrossed his legs, by way of shaking himself, recalled the charm and innocence of murderers he had known . . . and then composed his mind to the peace of a detective who has got his man. (p. 96)

As usual he forms an attachment for the accused and, also as usual, his attempts to ignore it make him harsher than he would be otherwise. Although more confident, Grant still questions his own motives.

He had yesterday changed his mind about going to the Clay funeral. The Tisdall evidence progressing normally, he had seen no need to give himself a harrowing hour which he could avoid. But only now did he realize how very glad he was to have escaped it, and (being Grant) began instantly to wonder whether after all he should have gone. Whether his subconscious desire to get out of it had influenced his decision. He decided that it had not. (p. 77)

Like Miss Pym in the next novel, he dislikes unpleasantness, yet feels guilty for avoiding it. It is interesting to note Grant's frequent ambivalence of feeling. He has, for example, almost paralyzing respect for Edward Champneis, yet realizes this is grossly unfair to the average, non-titled citizen. He, like Miss Pym, has a "looker-on" in him. And also, like Miss Pym, he makes incorrect, foolhardy, and dangerous assumptions. While this does add to the suspense, it also subtracts from Grant's character, suggesting he is at worst insensitive or at best merely unobservant. Furthermore, Tey's detectives seem without close friends and confidants. Although Grant shares some opinions with Williams, his assistant, his emotions are carefully hidden, even from himself.

Only when Erica, for example, states "It must have been awful for you" does Grant realize quite how awful it had been. Like Chandler's ideal detective in "The Simple Art of Murder," he is lonely, proud, and honorable by instinct. Like Wimsey, however, he is crammed with good intentions that often go astray. Aside from Grant, who is plagued by insecurity, Tey does not seem particularly kind to her characters. Tisdall is weak and foolish, at best wildly erratic. Jammy is persistent and annoying while Champneis is aloof and insensitive. Herbert, while not the most likable character, is drawn with a masterly touch. Tey, obviously more confident in her work, portrays Herbert adeptly, first through hearsay and opinion. Meg, Chris's friend from the lace factory, and Bundle the dresser describe and dislike the self-named "Brother of God." Tey sums up the American police report: "he had been jailed in Kentucky for blasphemy, in Texas for fraud, in Missouri for creating a riot, in Arkansas for his own safety and in Wyoming for seduction" (p. 166). Grant says of Herbert, "He certainly has all the stigmata: greed, enormous conceit, and lack of conscience. I rather hope he is our man. I would be doing the world a good turn to squash that slug" (p. 167).

III   *The Suspect Tisdall*

Tisdall, the suspect, is equally as significant as Grant in the novel. He shares with Lamont an irrational fear of the police and a tendency toward erratic behavior. Most of the other characters consider him "of no account," "weak," or "washy." Grant states, "Not enough guts to brazen a thing out. Not enough vanity, perhaps, to like the limelight at any price. Certainly the 'everyone sorry when I'm dead' type" (p. 95). Like Lamont, Tisdall has both opportunity and motive for the crime and all clues point directly toward him. Again like Lamont, he is innocent, hounded by the police, and becomes ill. There is little apparent rational motive for his actions and he seems closer to a breakdown than did Lamont.

IV   *The First Appearance of the Ingenue*

In *A Shilling for Candles* Tey uses, for the first time, the ingenuous, clever, witty young girl whose insight is far superior to adults in general and detectives in particular. Erica, the chief constable's daughter, is independent, intuitive, and determined. She can generally persuade others to acquiesce to her wishes. For example, she persuades Kindness, her Father's head groom, to loan her money.

"Oh, the car, is it?" he said jealously. Kindness hated Tinny [the car]. "If it's the car you want it for, why don't you ask Hart?"
"Oh, I couldn't." Erica was almost shocked. "Hart is quite new." Hart being a newcomer with only eleven years' service.
Kindness looked mollified.
"It isn't anything shady," she assured him. "I would have got it from Father at dinner tonight; the money, I mean; but he has gone to Uncle William's for the night. And women are so inquisitive," she added after a pause.
This, which could only refer to Nannie, made up the ground she had lost over the petrol. Kindness hated Nannie. (p. 119).

Erica, like Jane in *Brat Farrar*, dresses dowdily and is quite capable of managing her own affairs. Like Desterro in *Miss Pym Disposes*, her insights are penetrating and she speaks honestly and candidly. For example, she knows how Grant feels, before he is aware of it himself. Since Tey frequently uses this type of character, it is obvious that she is quite fond of the bright, aggressive girl as opposed to a sweet, quiet, and reserved one. Perhaps this is how she viewed herself or perhaps it was a desired ideal.

V   *Here Lies One Whose Name Was Writ in Water*

Again, as in *The Man in the Queue*, little can be said about the murderer. Keats, however, unlike Ray Marcable's mother, is alluded to several times in the novel and does make some brief appearances throughout the book. Nonetheless, her character is not as well drawn as that of Beau Nash in *Miss Pym Disposes*. Typically and according to tradition, Keats considers herself omnipotent and able to act without blame or punishment. She has a demonic pride and refuses to suffer. Her end is madness.

Undoubtedly there is obvious irony in her name. Keats, named after the poet who died young, causes a death by drowning and is herself drowned in insanity and pride. And, in case the reader misses the reference, Tey reminds:

The boy was turning from the shade of the entrance into the sunlit street. "Woman called Pope or something."

"Pope!" Jammy stood arrested halfway to the lift door. "You don't mean Keats, do you?"

"Is it Keats?" Musker looked at a card again. "Yes, so it is. I knew it was a poet . . ." (p. 181)

VI   *Tey's Character Craftmanship*

Tey indicates in this novel her deepening awareness of the less "important" characters in both the novel and life. Her so-called flat or minor characters are individual and memorable. Miss Pitts, for example, Clay's cook, is sensitively and realistically portrayed.

"What have you done with her—with the body, I mean?" she asked.

"At the mortuary."

This seemed to bring home tragedy for the first time.

"Oh, deary me." She moved the end of her apron over a polished table, slowly. "And me making griddle cakes."

This was not a lament for wasted griddle cakes, but her salute to the strangeness of life. (p. 21)

Tey is again evidencing the lessons she learned in stagecraft, both in character portrayal and in dialogue. In chapter 19, for example, Jammy's musings are characteristic and appropriate for a newsman.

That story about Clay's early days in the factory had been pure jam— even if that horse-faced dame HAD led him up the garden about knowing Chris, blast her. But you couldn't always rise to thrills or sobs, and if there was one emotion that the British public loved to wallow in it was being righteously indignant. So he, Jammy, had provided a wallow for them. The Yard knew quite well that tomorrow all these indignant people wouldn't remember a thing about it, so what the hell! What was there to get sore about? (p. 179)

Grant, on the other hand, speaks in a different voice.

He wished he was one of these marvellous creatures of superinstinct and infallible judgment who adored the pages of detective stories . . . As far as he could see, the obvious course is to interview one or the other of these men. And the obvious one to interview was Harmer. Why? Oh, because he'd talk more easily. Oh, yes, all right, and because there was less chance of running into trouble! (p. 231)

Here then, is reflected both the influence of her theatrical writing and a maturing of her fictional style.

VII   *The Misleading and the Misled*

Although Christine Clay, the victim, is ambitious, remote, and foolish, each character sees what he wants to in her. Detective Sergeant Williams, for example, sees her as vulnerable, having worked her way up from a lace factory (it should be noted that the sergeant himself had chosen to be "contented" rather than ambitious). Judy Sellers comments, "Not one of us cared a brass farthing for her. Most of us are tickled to death she's out of the way" (p. 64). Yet, Chris did will her ranch and five thousand pounds to give Tisdall a fresh start.

Often Tey portrays characters whose appearances are misleading. Tisdall, for example, seems weak and aimless, yet takes prompt and decisive action when he escapes. Judy Sellers, the actress is either mean and vindictive or kind and softhearted. "A bitch thinks all the world a bitch," Jammy states of her (p. 62), yet Grant later says of her, "Softhearted to the point of self-sacrifice" (p. 107).

There are only two major characters whom we see as stable, unsurprising, and unchanging, and they are emotional opposites. Grant, the reserved, often remote detective, carefully hides his emotions, even from himself. He remains constant and predictable. In this respect, he is similar to Miss Pym in Tey's next novel. Erica, the open, bright, sensitive "child," like Desterro in *Miss Pym Disposes*, is the opposite of the detective. She recognizes innocence, is aware both of her own emotions and others', and is fully equipped to confront an unstable, unreliable world.

Here then are both the conflict and theme. The characters are at odds both within and without; the world indeed is illusory with only one definite rule—no one can act with total impunity. Good or bad, actions must be paid for, as it were. By acting, a character reveals a glimpse of self preferably withheld and this, it seems, must somehow be punished. Erica acts to clear Tisdall and is attacked by a nasty old man and disliked by Grant. Lydia Keats's murders and her hidden avarice, cruelty, hatred, and madness are revealed, and she loses her fame and position.

Furthermore, none of the characters seem able to respond intimately or affectionately. Lord Edward Champneis, for example, the bereaved husband supposedly close to his wife, shows absolutely no emotion other than anger at Clay's fans. In fact, the author is very careful to point out a basic sexual purity in the characters. Tisdall says:

"Get this straight, Sergeant, and it may save you a lot of bother. Chris was my hostess. Not anything else. We stayed in her cottage unchaperoned, but a regiment of servants couldn't have made our relations more correct. Does that strike you as so very peculiar?"
   "Very," said the sergeant frankly. (p. 16)

Tey does not concern herself with an intimate, affectionate, man-woman relationship as Sayers, Allingham, Marsh and other female writers have done. Although she hints at occasional tender relationships (especially in later novels with Grant and Marta Hallard), never are they finely articulated. In fact, as in

Miss Pym, the female characters are loudly proclaimed virgins, in spite of temptation or suggestions otherwise.

In analyzing the novel, one can scarcely avoid words such as "suddenly," "abruptly," or "all at once." Tisdall is forever fainting, and characters fling themselves in and out of rooms without knocking, all in the best melodramatic manner. Exposition is provided by brief flashbacks or conversation. Furthermore, a heavier reliance on dialogue, not seen in *The Man in the Queue*, makes the narration both easier to follow and more memorable. Structurally, *A Shilling for Candles* is better than Tey's first novel. Several subplots, for example, add some suspense and give a deeper texture to the narration. While there is not the foreshadowing seen in *Miss Pym Disposes*, there is more preparation both for the climax and for the denouement. The author is applying the techniques learned in dramatic writing.

VIII   *Symbols and the Author's Philosophy*

The major symbols in the novel reflect the feeling that the world is a hostile place and that isolation while foolish is almost inevitable. The coat, for example, is both a protection (from cold and water) and a betrayer since it is on the evidence of the coat alone that Tisdall is hunted and the murderer is confronted.

The candles from the title suggest warmth, light, and religious security while in fact they are lighted by the fraudulent Brother Aloysius (Herbert). The monastery, in connection with this, is probably the most suggestive symbol. Tey obviously sees the monastic life as one of foolish isolation. "What did they shut out? Grant wondered. Life? Or were the bars to keep straying wills indoors?" (p. 207). Yet, Tisdall, Grant, and Clay all personify such isolation. They cannot respond honestly and openly on a personal basis with any other character. The isolated community is more fully developed in Tey's next novel, where Lucy Pym finds Leys Physical Training School both a comfort and a horror.

Finally, it should be noted that in her first three novels Tey's characters come to grief either by water, a hit on the head, or both. In *The Man in the Queue*, Lamont nearly dies from jumping into the river and getting hit on the head. Tisdall is made quite ill from exposure in a storm and Clay is killed by drowning. In *Miss*

Pym Disposes, Lucy notes the telltale footprints in the wet grass and Rouse is injured and later dies when the boom hits her head.

CHAPTER 6

Miss Pym Disposes

IN *Miss Pym Disposes* (1947), Tey temporarily discards the famous Inspector Grant and creates instead Miss Lucy Pym. Unlike Agatha Christie's Jane Marple or Patricia Wentworth's Miss Silver, Miss Pym is not a professional or semiprofessional detective. Rather, she is a retired mistress of French and author of a best-selling book on psychology. Not that she is a Freudian or Jungian by any means. Miss Pym is credited with writing a "basic text" on psychology for the layman—a 1930s version, perhaps, of *I'm OK, You're OK*. Thus is she separated, as far as the reader is concerned, from the intellectual elite. Lucy Pym never intended to write "the Book," as she calls it. Receiving a barely sufficient annuity from her one remaining parent, she retired from her teaching job. "She read on her first book on psychology out of curiosity, because it seemed to her an interesting sort of thing, and she read the rest to see if they were just as silly."[1] Lucy read thirty-seven "idiotic" volumes and proceeded to write pages of refutal. "Since one cannot talk about psychology in anything but jargon, there being no English for most of it, the reams of refutal read very learnedly indeed" (p. 7).

I *First Causes*

Because Henrietta Hodges, principal of Leys Physical Training College, had once stood up for her at school, Lucy feels obliged to lecture Henrietta's students on "her" subject. She discovers to her horror that the students' bell rings at 5:30 a.m., awakening them and her. Lucy hears one of the students, Dakers, shouting to Thomas for a safety pin. Characteristically, Thomas was still asleep. As the students dash to class, Lucy sinks back to sleep.

On her second awakening, Lucy determines to return to

London immediately after lunch. Beau Nash, one of the seniors, arrives and terms Lucy a "godsend" in the claustrophobic, grim lives of the students. In the bathroom, two other seniors, Dakers, the girl with the missing safety pin, and O'Donnell also assume Lucy is staying for the tea. Being weak and frankly flattered by the girls' enthusiasm and attention, Miss Pym remains at Leys.

Since Saturday is "match day," all the students with the exception of Teresa Desterro are at the games. Though preferring to be alone in this quiet, Eden-like atmosphere, Lucy is kept company by the Brazilian "Nut Tart" who appears to have the best insight into the student body. They are not "Nice, clean, healthy children" as Lucy wishes to believe (p. 24). "They are very naive, the English girls. They are like little boys of nine" (p. 27).

Everything is e-norrmously exaggerated. Everyone is just the least bit insane. No, it is true, I promise you. If a student is frightened by nature, then she is a thousand times more frightened this term. If she is ambitious, then her ambition becomes a passion. . . . It is not a normal life they lead. You cannot expect them to be normal. (p. 30)

Refusing to believe the Nut Tart's summation of characters and emotions, Lucy delights in the "sunburnt alertness" of the seniors at their tea.

The only face that approached distinction, as opposed to good looks, was that of Mary Innes, Beau Nash's Jonathan . . . Not that Innes was particularly good looking. Her eyebrows, low over her eyes, gave her face an intensity, a brooding expression, that robbed her fine bones of the beauty they might have had. (p. 32) . . . It was round faces like Mary Innes's that history was built. (p. 33)

At the tea Lucy also meets Rouse, disliked by the other girls, cool and remote. The students explain about the "Dem," a sort of physical prowess program which they put on at the end of the year. This exposition slows the pace of thought and action for Lucy, while emphasizing the tension, fear, and emotion in the students. They also discuss the "Post Lottery" or job assignments. "The most agonising moment of the whole term [is] when [the students] are summoned to Miss Hodges' room and told what . . . [their] fate is going to be" (p. 37). These two elements plus the threat of examinations contribute to the tension and suffocating atmosphere as the weeks pass.

After supper that evening, Lucy learns of the two "college crimes," using the gym as a shortcut to the playing fields and food pilfering. Neither of these are accurate as the reader later discovers. The college crime is in fact exaggerated ambition as seen in both Rouse and Innes as well as Henrietta. It all leads finally to "accidental" murder. And, though Henrietta dislikes admitting it, there are "accidents" and "breakdowns." While the staff is in part responsible for the pressure on the students, they generally have a fond and tolerant feeling toward them, and like to stress their normality. "We are an unsensational crowd" (p. 43), comments Madame Lefevre the dancing mistress. Ironically, Miss Wragg, one of the gymnasts, adds: "Too normal by half . . . A little spot of scandal would be nice now and again. A nice change from hand-stands and upward circlings" (p. 43). As the staff continues to discuss the "Dem" and various time tables, Dr. Knight, the medical lecturer, asks Miss Pym to take her psychology lecture on Thursday. She wishes to attend a conference. Lucy agrees, delighting in the fact that the students enjoy her. She is also intrigued by the assignment of posts to the students and of "a plum," "a really wonderful chance for someone" (p. 48). Again, a note of anxiety and tension is sounded by Miss Lux, foreshadowing the crime:

It is when one is as tired as that that one's emotional state ceases to be normal. A tiny obstacle becomes an Everest in the path; a careless comment becomes a grievance to be nursed; a small disappointment is all of a sudden a suicidal affair. (p. 49)

These thoughts echo those of Desterro, and again Lucy refuses to believe that the girls are anything but laughing and happy. The following morning in Henrietta's office, Lucy overhears mention of a letter from Arlinghurst, "a sort of female Eton," and assumes correctly that it is the "plum" Henrietta is hugging to herself. Protesting again that the college crime was cutting through the gym, Henrietta takes Lucy on a tour of the gymnasium, pointing out "The Abhorrence," the powerful vacuum that will later play such an important role in the discovery of the murderer. Lucy insists "There is something

obscene about it" (p. 56), as indeed there will be, when it helps
point to the crime and the suspected criminal. Watching the girls
practice, Lucy notes that Innes's face is "Sixteenth century,
rather. Withdrawn, uncompromising, unforgiving; the stake-or-
nothing" (p. 58). Ironically, as the reader later discovers, this is
both a true and a false character judgment. For while Innes is
these things, Beau is even more so, under a benevolent surface.
Innes, on the other hand, is sensitive, responsible, and forgiving—which Beau can never be.

Lucy also notices Miss Rouse.

There was no fooling about for Miss Rouse; life was real, life was
earnest; life was long hamstrings and a good post in the offing. Lucy
wished she liked Miss Rouse better. . . . (p. 58)

Yet, she does feel sorry for her when Rouse freezes on the
booms.

In strained silence Rouse sprang to the boom and began her progress
along it. For half its length she performed with professional expertness,
and then for no apparent reason her hand missed the boom as she
turned and her body swung away, suspended by her other hand. She
made an effort to recover herself, pulling up with her sustaining hand,
but the rhythm was broken and she dropped to her feet. (p. 61)

Noticing the expression on Henrietta's face as she watches the
girls, Lucy feels pangs of jealousy. "Henrietta had built for
herself a life that was full, rich and satisfying" (p. 60). Henrietta,
stubborn, pompous, narrow-minded, and obsessive, has a lifelong
love affair with the school. Only her unusual attachment and
sympathy for Rouse blinds her vision. Lucy suggests that the
principal projects her own feelings of inadequacy, lovelessness,
and plainness upon Rouse. Yet, she cannot agree with the
principal that Rouse is "one of our most brilliant students" (p.
62). Lucy dislikes the girl even more when she notices Rouse
"being smarmy . . . laying it on with the trowel" (p. 65) when
speaking to Henrietta. Again the sense of pressure and fatigue is
emphasized as Lucy walks past one of the classrooms: "Gone was
the excitement, the flush of exercise . . . Gone for the moment
was even the youth. The faces were tired and spiritless" (p. 66).

On Wednesday during final exam week, Desterro invites Lucy
to the village for coffee. A handsome, happy couple, obviously of

straitened means, enter the tea shop and ask for griddle cakes so loved by their daughter at Leys. After a moment Lucy recognizes them as Innes's parents. They are merely passing through on the way to a conference and don't wish to disturb their daughter during finals. Desterro comments that Innes is beautiful. This proves to be true of Innes's inner self as well as her outward appearance later in the novel. In private, Desterro adds that Innes reminds her of her "great-grandmother's grandmother" whose "husband died too conveniently" (p. 79). It is in the tea shop that Lucy first wonders about "first causes," that is, how one action leads inevitably to another and another into the future.

Since Miss Lux is overburdened with exam papers, Lucy offers to monitor the senior pathology final for her. Suddenly she notices Rouse looking furtive.

> She had not been Form Mistress of the Lower Fourth for nothing. Every eater of illicit sweets wore that expression. So did those who were doing their arithmetic in French lesson. So did those who were cheating at an examination. (p. 82)

Uncertain about what to do, she decides that instead of upsetting the seniors at their least stable moment, she would only see to it that Rouse cheats no more. This error in judgment is one of the "first causes" of the crime. Had Rouse been apprehended, she never would have gotten that Arlinghurst post. Rouse then has an obviously difficult time. After the exam, Lucy walks toward the fields past the gym and discovers, dropped in the grass, a tiny address book with pathology notes in it. Apparently it had been used by someone to cheat in an examination. This, of course, foreshadows the later discovery of the rosette, again assumed at first to belong to Rouse.

Instead of going to Henrietta and upsetting her, and since ownership of the book could not be proved, only suspected, Lucy drops it into the stream. Again, Lucy acts wrongly with the best of intentions. Life, she felt, would be one of perpetual doubt for the evil doer, not knowing what had become of the book. On returning to school, Lucy notes that Rouse "who found written work so difficult" (p. 91) had made three firsts, while Innes got honors in her exams. Nonetheless, Lucy still believes:

It was absurd to think of them as harassed adults, trembling on the precipice edge of breakdown. They were volatile children; their griefs were loud and vocal, and transient. (pp. 92–93)

Suspense is built as both Thomas and Dakers are assigned posts and no mention is made of Arlinghurst. In fact, it is the students who first whisper about "the plum." All assume Innes will get the post. Innes, meanwhile, looks as if she were "seeing Heaven opened" (p. 99). Her wildest dreams appear to be on the verge of fulfillment. Lucy, deciding to hear what the staff's reaction will be, goes to the drawing room and abruptly discovers herself in the midst of a staff row.

A row, moreover, if one was to judge from the faces, of most unholy proportions. Henrietta was standing, flushed and defensive and stubborn, with her back to the fireplace, and the others were staring at her, accusing and angry. (p. 100)

Henrietta has decided to give Rouse the Arlinghurst position. The staff disagrees wholeheartedly, insisting "What will matter then is character. And what Miss Rouse has of character is neither very much nor very admirable" (p. 102). Henrietta, however, is adamant.

My position as a minority may not be very strong, Miss Lux, but my position as Principal of this college is unquestioned, and what you think or do not think of my decisions is immaterial. I took you into my confidence, as I always have, about the disposal of this vacancy. That you do not agree with me is, of course regrettable, but of no consequence. It is for me to make decisions here and in this case I have made it. (p. 103–104)

The staff realizes irritably that they are helpless. "My good if tactless Catherine," Madame said, rising gracefully to her feet, "all we can do is go to our rooms and pray" (p. 105). Lucy, hoping that the principal is not sure of her own position, decides to confront her with the tale of Rouse's cheating. Henrietta, as expected, explains away the evidence as circumstantial.

At supper that evening, Lux admits acquaintance with Edward Adrian, the Shakespearean actor appearing in town:

He went to school with my brother. . . . A very horrid little boy. . . .

A quite revolting little boy. Always watching himself in mirrors. And possessed of a remarkable talent for getting the best of everything that was going. (pp. 119–120)

Frankly she is more concerned with reminding Lucy to bring the staff a few tidbits from the students' parties to which she is invited. Lucy is personally not looking forward to the occasion as it will probably mean seeing Innes. At Stewart's, Daker's, and Thomas's party that evening Lucy learns that Rouse is still practicing on the boom and will be till the day of the demonstration so that she doesn't lose her nerve again. Happily, Beau and Innes are at the theater, so Lucy is spared the agony of seeing the momentarily happy girl. Rouse, also fortunately, is not invited. O'Donnell, one of the few girls without a post, arrives late at the party, casual, but suspiciously bright-eyed. There is no doubt that the affair of "Post Lottery" is deadly serious for all the girls.

The day of the inevitable announcement of Rouse's position Lucy wishes she had had the foresight to invent a luncheon engagement and remove "herself out of the area of the explosion that was coming" (p. 127). She speaks with Desterro before lunch and is told all about Rick, the Nut Tart's distant cousin and apparent boy friend. "By ones and twos, and in little groups, the students returned from their compulsory hour out of College" (p. 130). Beau and Innes are the last to arrive and Lucy guiltily begs out of afternoon tea with the seniors, knowing only too well what the atmosphere will be. Lucy wishes to "run away from unpleasantness like a child. Not for the first time, she wished she was a more admirable character" (p. 131).

The staff is still irritated and upset about Henrietta's decision. Madame, however, insists

My good, if too earnest, Catherine, you must learn to take life as it comes, and to withdraw yourself from what you cannot alter. As the Chinese so rightly advise: When rape is inevitable relax and enjoy it. We connive at an abomination, as you so exquisitely put it. True. But as intelligent human beings we concern ourselves with the by-products of the action. It will be interesting to see how, for instance, the little Innes reacts to the stimulus. Will the shock be a mortal one, will it galvanize her into action, or will it send her into crazy throes of galvanic activity that has no meaning? (p. 132)

Actually, of course, it is Beau who is "galvanized" into activity.
After lunch, Rouse is summoned to Henrietta's office to be
offered to the Arlinghurst post. At this point the tension reaches
a climax. All that remains then is to resolve the dilemmas and
emotions aroused by Henrietta's foolhardy gesture.

Lucy leaves the grounds immediately after lunch, hoping to
escape most of the upheaval.

She would go away deep into the green and white and yellow
countryside, and smell the hay and lie in the grass and feel the world
turning on its axis, and remember that it was a very large world, and
that College griefs were wild and bitter but soon over and that in the
Scale of Things they were undeniably Very Small Beer. (p. 137)

Unfortunately, she meets Beau who angrily accuses her of
cruelty. Innes should have been warned; she is terribly hurt.
Lucy's naiveté and illusions are still intact as she sees Beau as "a
child raging and hurt at the wrong that had been done her friend.
Lucy had never liked her so well" (p. 139). Again she ignores the
possibilities of this friendship and Beau's character. Beau
continues to search for the missing Innes, the girl who "cared too
much about things. . . . She had no oil on her feathers, Innes"
(p. 140).

Finally, making her way to the tea shop in town, Lucy meets
Desterro and Rick who have not heard about Innes's disaster.
The Nut Tart is irate, seeing it as a terrible insult. Rick is both
kind and understanding.

That night, Lucy hears no sound from Innes's room, and the
following day is anticlimactic. Everyone is "talked out" and the
college proceeds as usual preparing for the demonstration. The
entire week in fact is quiet except for two incidents. Innes turns
down a post at an orthopaedic hospital and it goes to O'Donnell,
and Edward Adrian arrives to see Lux. Lucy is immediately
snared by Catherine to keep her company and avoid being alone
with Adrian. A theater party is arranged for after the "Dem."
Here, then, is the first hint that Lucy's character judgment is not
as good as she imagined. Lux is not "an unwanted plain woman
who found compensation in life by devoting herself to a beautiful
young sister. She was a potentially attractive creature who so
little needed compensation that she couldn't be bothered with
one of the most successful and handsome men in the world

today" (p. 157). This foreshadows Lucy's realization in the final chapter that "As a psychologist . . . she was a very good teacher of French" (p. 157).

At lunch on Thursday, Lucy is shocked by Innes's "burnt up inside" appearance. She reminds Miss Pym of "one of those apparently perfect things that collapse into dust at a touch because they are hollow inside" (p. 159). In addition to the shame and injustice of losing Arlinghurst, it appears that Innes will have no post at all. After she turned down Henrietta's offer of the orthopaedic hospital, the college will not help her further with a job search. Most of all, Lucy feels sorry for "Innes's barren tomorrow" (p. 161), the time when she must face her proud and hopeful parents. Ironically, this phrase aptly sums the scope of Innes's future and all the barren tomorrows thereafter. Lucy pleads with Henrietta to help get Innes a job "before five o'clock this afternoon" and is rebuked for being "extraordinarily impulsive and frivolous" (p. 162).

Lucy awakens early on "Dem Day" with a delicious feeling of excitement. She decides to go for an early stroll, and notices that the "faint damp marks of her [Rouse's] gym shoes are visible on the concrete path" (p. 166). Rouse, she assumes, has been practicing her routine just once more. In the gym, Lucy notices a small rosette, flat and silvery, on the floor. Absently she picks it up, reminded of the party shoes to which such a rosette belonged. Since the gym had already been cleaned by "the Abhorrence," the ornament must have dropped off Rouse's shoe.

Later at breakfast, Henrietta notices that Rouse is missing. Juniors and staff search for her, and she is found in the gym with a fractured skull. The pin in the boom was improperly fastened and fell on her head. Apparently either Rouse or O'Donnell, who helped her put it up, was at fault. O'Donnell, however, did not put up the end that fell. The principal and staff assume that either Rouse was at fault or some unknown vibration jarred the pin loose. During prayers, Lucy suddenly wonders whose footprints she saw and whose rosette she picked up.

The students rehearse frantically to try to make up for one missing in their number, and Innes is immediately offered Arlinghurst since Rouse would be quite incapacitated. Lucy worries and agonizes over the mysterious footprints and ornament. On packing Rouse's things, Lucy discovers no shoe. Knowing she must confront Henrietta with the evidence, Lucy suffers an agony of indecision and self-contempt. Innes is seen walking with her parents. She looks at peace, though still upset. Delaying action, Lucy watches the girls perform. During the "Dem," however, Innes freezes on the boom and cannot continue. Furthermore, during the remainder of the performance, she acts as if she were trying to kill herself. As the guests move to the lawn, Lucy meets Beau's parents. They again suggest Nash's stubborn selfishness. She had held a sit-down strike at the age of four in order to get her way. The preparation for the final revelation of Beau's character is carefully executed. Lucy's firm belief in Nash's normality is a case of protesting too much.

The seniors perform their dance, and Lucy speaks with Desterro's Rick. She vaguely suggests her dilemma and he, like Madame, suggests, "Let God dispose" (p. 189). "Man proposes God disposes," but in this case, it becomes Lucy Pym who disposes in a godlike way, and allows murder and injustice to triumph.

Edward Adrian joins Lucy and asks after Innes who has "a wonderful face. Pure Borgia" (p. 191). Once tea is over, Lucy persuades Lux to accompany Adrian to the after-theater party. She has a convenient headache. Miss Pym and Rick watch the dancing which is dull and uninspired until the Nut Tart appears. She is enchanting, brilliant, and nearly professional. Supper is subdued both because of exhaustion and the recollection of Rouse's "accident." Afterwards Lucy is invited to the common room by the students and notices to her horror that the ornament is missing off one of Innes's shoes. Then, quite unexpectedly, the news comes of Rouse's death.

That night, unable to sleep, Lucy ponders on the problem. She should of course, go at once to Henrietta with the evidence. "Do the obvious right thing . . . and let God dispose" (p. 189), Rick had said. And it had seemed a sensible ruling. What, she asks herself, is justice?

To break a woman's heart; to bring ruin and shame on Henrietta and the destruction of all she had built up; to rub out forever the radiance of Beau, the Beau, who was unconditioned to grief. Was that a life for a life? That was three—no, four lives for one. (p. 203)

Hopefully, Lucy thinks that Innes will provide her own punishment. Ironically, she will, though innocent of the actual crime. Once again Lucy wonders about "first causes."

The operative cause was Innes's vulnerability. But the button that has set the whole tragedy in motion was pressed by Henrietta.

And now she, Lucy, was waiting to press another button which would set in motion machinery even more monstrous. Machinery that would catch up in its gears and meshes, and maim and destroy, the innocent with the guilty. (p. 205)

Finally she sees herself as an unwilling instrument of the Deity.

If God did dispose—as undoubtedly He did in the latter end—then perhaps the disposing was already at work. Had begun when it was she and not someone else who found the little rosette. . . . It had been found by a feeble waverer like herself, who could never see less than three sides to any question. (p. 206)

Yet she cannot break the law either. Resolving finally not to suppress evidence, she falls into an uneasy sleep.

In the gray and sodden morning, Lucy confronts Innes. The girl does not deny Lucy's accusation.

". . . I understand that there is only one pair of those old-fashioned pumps in College."

There was silence, Lucy laid the little object down on the table and waited.

"Am I wrong?" she asked at last.

"No." (p. 209)

At this point, Tey does not "play fair" with the reader. Lucy insists "there is only one pair of those old-fashioned pumps in College" (p. 209), information obtained from unknown sources. Since apparently everyone had such shoes at one time, it is very doubtful that everyone would have disposed of their shoes. It is indeed difficult to accept the coincidence that Innes and Nash were the only two to own such shoes, and both have one ornament missing.

Innes insists:

". . . It wasn't meant to be—. I know you'll think I'm just trying to white-wash it, but it was never meant to be—to be the way it turned out. It was because I was so sick about missing Arlinghurst—I practically lost my reason over that for a time—I behaved like an idiot. It got so that I couldn't think of anything in the world but Arlinghurst. And this was just to be a way of—of letting me have a second chance at it. It was never meant to be more than that. (p. 109)

Lucy, admitting she cannot decide what to do, states, "Of course you cannot possibly be allowed to profit by Rouse's death" (p. 210). Innes offers to spend the rest of her life "atoning for yesterday morning" (p. 210). She will return and work with her father although, "My one ambition since I was a little girl has been to get away from living in a little market town; coming to Leys was my passport to freedom" (p. 211). Lucy persuades herself to accept this. She cannot send anyone to the gallows. Innes breaks down and sobs.

Here again is one recurring theme in Tey: mistaken identity. Innes is mistaken for Nash as the criminal, and Nash's characteristics are mistakenly seen in Innes.

Lucy decides to leave Leys once the diplomas have been presented. The students give her small gifts and she is invited to the Nut Tart's wedding to Rick. Beau helps her pack and discovers the rosette.

> "That looks like the little button thing off my shoe." she said.
> "YOUR shoe?"
> "Yes. . . . So this is where I lost it." (p. 223)

Lucy is shocked.

She wondered why she had never noticed before how "cold those blue eyes were. Brilliant and cold and shallow" (p. 223). And Miss Pym, her illusions stripped away, returns to London. "As a psychologist she was a first-rate teacher of French" (p. 224).

II *Lucy and Her World*

Lucy Pym is, in some respects, in the tradition of the spinster detectives. She lives alone, likes it, and is apparently well adjusted. She is unmarried, and she does solve a crime. However, here the resemblance ends. Unlike her strong-minded sisters, Lucy is weak-willed, self-indulgent, and self-punishing, a silly woman, aware of her own shortcomings but with sincere and sensitive feelings. Her illusions and naiveté make her more realistic than other female detectives. For example, she judges by appearance alone—Innes's nature is determined and ambitious because she has "level eyebrows" (p. 75) and Beau is "a goddess" because she has blond hair and blue eyes. Assuming the girls to be "Nice clean, healthy children" (p. 24), she is shocked to discover the truth. Then too, her decisions are faulty for the best of motives. For example, she does not call Rouse down for cheating for fear of upsetting the other girls. Lucy Pym is capable of seeing two sides to every question. Again, she feels sorry for Rouse because she must cheat, but heartily dislikes her for it. (The reader cannot help but ask if Lucy would have been as tolerant and fair-minded if Rouse had killed Innes or Nash.)

Finally, it should be stressed that Lucy is not first and foremost a detective. In fact, her inaccurate character judgments and inattention to details make her a poor detective indeed. The novel, incidentally, is more concerned with character revelation than actual detection, which occurs almost by accident in the sixteenth chapter.

Lucy's world is one of enviable protection and isolation. Although there is some vague mention of lectures and publishers' receptions, she seems quite out of contact with reality. Her arrival at Leys intensifies this isolation, putting her into a limited and essentially self-sufficient society, "like a convent," Nash says. Lucy adds, "Only the self-absorption was the same; the narrowness" (p. 40).

The village apparently consists mainly of a warm, cozy tea shop specializing in delicious treats and run by a happy motherly woman. The school itself is staffed by dedicated, competent women devoted to their institution. All are well adjusted and without defensive apology for their spinsterhood. Men, rarely considered at all, are generally regarded as tedious, self-centered, and boring. For the instructors, then, the atmosphere is undeniably cloister-like. Henrietta assumes the role of mother superior who governs absolutely. The students are novices; they work and are worked to exhaustion, and none is ever involved in mischief, pranks, or games. It is perhaps revealing to note that none of these "typical" English girls has a beau, nor is marriage considered a possibility. Aside from Desterro who is "a foreigner" (and that, it appears, explains all types of unusual behavior), there is a surprising lack of interest in men.

The tension and competition, then, do not have an overt sexual basis, although repression takes its toll. Instead, the sources are grades and posts. Furthermore, this tension among the students is, so to speak, "All clean fun." No girl is basically cruel, avaricious, mean, amoral, or immoral. Real crime cannot occur, only a premeditated "accident" with devastating results.

III *Style*

In *Miss Pym Disposes,* Tey's promising ability for characterization reaches fulfillment. In chapter 3, for example, Tey characterizes the entire staff in a few short lines.

Miss Lux—angular, plain and clever—was Mistress of Theory and as befitted a lecturer on theory had not only ideas but opinions. Miss Wragg, on the other hand, the Junior Gymnast—bit, bouncing, young and pink—had apparently no ideas at all and her only opinions were reflections of Madame Lefevre's. Madame Lefevre, the ballet mistress, spoke seldom, but when she did it was in a voice like dark brown velvet and no one interrupted her. At the bottom of the table, with her mother by her side, sat Froken Gustavsen, the Senior Gymnast, who talked not at all. (p. 23)

From this point on, the author merely adds flesh to these bones. The fact that we see these characters through Lucy's often clouded and naive vision adds to the reader's insight, both of Miss Pym and the school.

Aside from characterization, Tey in this novel masters the art of foreshadowing. She combines this with the detective novel's "red herrings" in a carefully designed structure that leads inevitably to the shocking conclusion. For example, the first real element of foreshadowing occurs in chapter 3 when Desterro insists that life at Leys is not normal, in fact "e-norrrmously exaggerated" (p. 30). She also suggests characteristics in Nash that should prepare the reader for the final discovery of guilt.

She is a strong-minded creature, and so has suffered less, perhaps. But would you call her friendship for Innes quite normal? *Nice,* of course . . . quite irreproachable. But normal, no. (p. 29)

Again, Lucy points out "it was around faces like Mary Innes's that history was built" (p. 33), a statement which is both ironic and a "red herring." If we are to believe that Innes commits the crime, when in fact she is guilty of only unconscious inspiration, we must be prepared by such statements as Desterro's comparison of

Innes to an ancestor whose "husband died too conveniently" (p. 79).

External conflicts between individuals are not nearly as significant in this novel as internal conflicts. In this respect, Tey writes in the best tradition of Dorothy L. Sayers, and, though she would surely be the last to admit it, Raymond Chandler. Lucy is of course in constant conflict with herself. Henrietta, too, tries to appear unprejudiced among her students, but in truth adores the "smarmy" Rouse. The most pitiable conflict, however, is Innes's since it is both unrecognized and ignored. She must surrender her hopes, ambition, and desires to pay for the crime of her friend. She cannot tolerate failure in herself and is extremely self-demanding; yet to atone for the crime of Beau and her own part, however subtle and unrecognized, she sacrifices her life. Her feelings of guilt and the fear that she somehow inspired her friend to crime will haunt her until her death.

The overriding symbol in the novel is undoubtedly "The Abhorrence," the powerful vacuum in the gym. "Nature abhors a vacuum," states Henrietta, yet this is exactly the atmosphere at Leys. Cut off, isolated, in a vacuum, events get out of proportion, expand to fill the emptiness, and destroy the lives of two girls. The lives of the students are abnormal and abhorrent—the strain and pressure causing accidents and breakdowns. Yet, as Lucy says, the Abhorrence is "Terrible and fascinating" (p. 64). Perhaps this justly sums up life at Leys.

A second symbol is the rosette—an ornament off a party shoe, a symbol of youth and gaiety dropped after the Abhorrence had done its work. It reveals both the second victim of the crime, Innes, and the criminal, Beau. The rosette ironically symbolizes happiness, indicating, then, the end of Mary Innes's hopes, the beginning of her "barren tomorrows."

IV   *Theme*

In chapter 7 Lucy asks herself, "What were first causes anyhow?" It is an unanswerable question, both when Lucy asks it first and at the end of the novel. Lucy suggests that Henrietta's decision was the first cause for the murder, but undoubtedly the characters of Innes and Beau were also at fault. Lucy's own decisions to ignore Rouse's cheating and destroy the small red book were also influential.

Here too, Tey again employs the theme of conflict between surface and inner reality. What appears to be a certainty in terms of character expectations is in fact entirely false. The innocent appears guilty while the criminal seems a "nice, healthy" girl. The same is true of other characters: Adrian appears a poised man about town and is in fact a vain if sometimes sincere child. Lux, as previously discussed, appears to be a plain, lonely woman when in fact she is not. Again and again this theme recurs in Tey, suggesting that the author herself might have found life and individuals disconcerting, untrustworthy, and emotionally dangerous. Or perhaps the author sensed that she herself was not really as other people saw her and considered other individuals equally deceptive—surely a rational viewpoint in the postwar period.

V   The Tradition

Miss Pym Disposes belongs to the "escapist" mode of literature. That is, all events in the real world, war, strikes, political upheavals, etc., are totally ignored. Crime is essentially accidental, and there are no bloody corpses scattered around. The society is a closed one and basically innocent. The novel fits loosely into the detective mode, albeit with an unwilling detective. The crime, however, is not solved by deduction, but by an admission of guilt similar to *The Man in the Queue*. Here, however, with the intensive use of foreshadowing and the large and essential role of Beau in the basic action, the preparation is satisfactory for the denouement. Miss Pym with all her foibles and self-doubts is sensitively and realistically portrayed. Further, in spite of the large number of characters, the reader is never confused because of the careful craftsmanlike descriptions and dialogue which delineate each character.

Miss Pym Disposes is in many respects similar to Dorothy L. Sayers' *Gaudy Night*, published in 1936. The action in both novels is limited to a scholastic setting. In *Gaudy Night*, the crimes occur in a women's college at Oxford, a location with which Sayers was most familiar. Tey's novel is set at Leys College of Physical Training, again an all-female institution similar no doubt to the school at which Miss Mackintosh was trained. Both authors approach and analyze the problems and pressure of the cloister-type life. For Tey, the pressures are physical as well as mental and emotional. The girls, worked to exhaustion in preparation for their demonstration, are also subjected to intense and difficult written testing. Finally, their general uncertainty regarding job possibilities and assignments creates an atmosphere of nervous hysteria. It is in this pressure cooker, then, that murder occurs.

The emphasis in *Gaudy Night*, however, is more intellectual and emotional. Sayers deals with the sensitivities and reactions of unmarried women scholars, all of whom are extremely defensive. Whereas none of Tey's characters feel they have trespassed in a male sanctuary, or must apologize for their spinsterhood, Sayers' scholars are constantly aware that they are acting in a so-called "unwomanly manner." They often feel obliged to explain away their interest in scholarship as well as their unmarried state. The Warden and Dean are accused of overcompensating when dealing with a menial who "has a family to support." This in fact inspires the crimes since the criminal, a scout or maid named Annie Wilson, feels "a woman's place is in the home."

Both authors emphasize the isolation of the academic community. This, of course, is in complete accord with W. H. Auden's prescription for a detective novel in "The Guilty Vicarage."[2] The society must be closed, that is, have a limited and specific number. It must appear to be an innocent society, and the characters should be both eccentric and good. Often there is elaborate ritual in this society, and the criminal uses knowledge of this ritual to commit the crime or crimes. Aside from the church and formal affairs of state, few things are more ritualistic than the activities of a university or college with the hierarchy of administrators and scholars, gowns or particular dress, the senior common room, studying, testing, and graduation. Dorothy L. Sayers' novel fits Auden's requirements slightly better since the atmosphere of Oxford is, at first, Edenic. The atmosphere at Leys is anything but. In fact, it is more like a nightmare with the raucous bells, shouting, hurrying students, and abnormal pressure. It is unusual to find such a strong sense of fear and pressure *before* the crime occurs. Tey spends two-thirds of the novel building up the suspense and pressure. The accident/murder is almost anticlimactic. Most writers of mystery and detective fiction and Tey in her earlier novels execute the crime almost at once and then proceed to build suspense and suspicion. In this respect, *Miss Pym Disposes* is unique.

Both Sayers and Tey begin, then, by establishing atmosphere. Sayers quickly turns to the first hints of the poison pen attacks. Tey slowly, deftly, and painstakingly creates the atmospheric tension and characterization that make this novel interesting and unusual.

Tey and Sayers both use female detectives. Miss Pym and Harriet Vane share an interest in and fondness for the staff and students. Both are sensitive and prone to self-analysis and self-torture. Harriet can neither forget her trial nor forgive Peter Wimsey for saving her life. Lucy, on a far more mundane level, agonizes over revealing the truth about Rouse's death and over her responsibility for silence. Harriet, while vaguely sorry for Annie when her crimes are revealed, is more concerned with the innocence of the scholastic community. Lucy, on the other hand, is deeply shocked and concerned over both the crime and the criminal. While both Lucy and Harriet are writers, it does seem odd that Lucy should be the author of a psychological book, while Harriet, the intellectual, specializes in mystery fiction. The criminals in each novel are equally egocentric, stubborn, and obsessive. Each is certain of her rightness and assumes that no blame or punishment can or will be exacted. In both novels there is a case of mistaken identity—an innocent appears guilty, while it seems impossible for the real criminal to be responsible.

Finally, there is a strong pro-feminist theme in both novels, though perhaps pro-individual would be a better word. Each author feels that a person should do whatever it is he or she does best, as Sayers puts it, regardless of sex. More muted in Tey, the emphasis is on the ability to survive in an indifferent if not hostile environment. Innes will survive—my life for hers—and so of course will Lucy without male help or domination, it is implied.

What then is the appeal of this type of novel? Crime occurs in a safe, isolated, well-run society. Everything is neat, clean, and orderly. There are generally plenty of good books, sherry, cocoa, servants, and likeable characters. No one is really ever ill, diseased, schizophrenic, dirty, or evil. The victim seems either unreal, unpleasant, or both. There is always some grain of sympathy for the criminal who often acts from essentially noble motivation. Though murder occurs, there is no blood and none of the violence characteristic of Chandler or Hammett. Our detective suffers perhaps more than the criminal for solving the crime. And thus she seems more sympathetic than say Nero

Wolfe or Hercule Poirot for whom the solution is more a mental exercise than an emotional involvement. These novels offer the reader a sense of security and stability in a threatening and unstable world.

CHAPTER 7

Brat Farrar

*B**RAT** Farrar (1949)*[1] is Tey's second novel without Inspector Grant. As in *Miss Pym Disposes* (1947), her previous novel, Brat Farrar is neither a professional nor semiprofessional detective. Ironically, he is a criminal who becomes involved initially because of his own greed and later because of his interest in and affection for the family involved. Once again the reader discovers Tey's beloved ingenue, this time divided into twins. One twin is neat and Desterro-like while the other is ragged and resembles Erica in *A Shilling for Candles* (1936). Aunt Bee, guardian of the girls and their elder sister and brother, herself bears a remarkable resemblance to Lucy Pym. The setting, too, resembles in substance if not form that of *Miss Pym Disposes.* The estate, like Leys Physical Training School, is isolated, protected, beautiful, and secure at the beginning of the action. Latchetts, as it is named, has been held together by the raising and selling of horses. Once again, then, Tey stresses the physical rather than intellectual approach to life as seen for example in the works of Dorothy L. Sayers.

I   *The Plot*

Tey's approach to both exposition and foreshadowing in the first several chapters is at once more refined and artistic than in her previous works and shows strongly the influence of dramatic techniques. Rapidly the background is sketched in, first through Aunt Bee's musing, and then through conversation with the rector's wife, an old and valued technique of the well-made play.

Aunt Bee had cared for the children for eight years since the death of her brother and his wife. Times had been difficult and money short. In six weeks, however, Simon, the eldest son, will inherit his mother's fortune, and all will be well. Bee does have some well-founded doubts about Simon, however.

There were times when she had—no, not been afraid. Times perhaps when she had wondered. Simon had far too many sides to him; a quicksilver quality that did not go with a yeoman inheritance.

Ironically she adds:

Here and there came a ne'er-do-well—like her cousin Walter—but Providence had seen to it that the worthless quality had been confined to younger sons, who could practise their waywardness on subjects remote from Latchetts. (p. 9)

As the reader later discovers, Pat, the dead twin, was in fact the eldest son. Simon is worthless and Walter, contrary to Bee's opinion, had a worthwhile son in Brat.

The vicar's attractive wife Nancy, once both famous and wealthy, continues the exposition by asking, "What became of cousin Walter?" (p. 13). Bee replies, "Oh, he died. . .Even Walter wasn't bad, you know. He just liked drink and hadn't the head for it" (pp. 13-14). Bee again recalls the deaths of Bill and Nora, the children's parents, and this, of course, brings to mind the death of Patrick, Simon's twin brother. The use of twins and identical cousins, and the confusions they cause, is a famous and well-worn dramatic device used to best advantage in Shakespeare. In Tey, however, the device seems more a splitting and dividing of personalities into opposite and controllable parts. Simon is irresponsible and dangerous; Pat, it appears, was good and kind. "Simon had a careless generosity when it did not cost him inconvenience; but Patrick had had that inner kindness that not only gives but gives up" (p. 15).

The traits of both Simon and Patrick are then recombined in Brat, Patrick's double, who is both criminal and angel. On a more obvious level, Ruth and Jane are neat opposites; clean, orderly and well-dressed as opposed to messy, sloppy, and ragamuffin.

Pat had drowned at the age of thirteen, apparently a suicide since he left a farewell note to Bee. His aunt reasons:

I think that it was all too much for Patrick; too strange. The adrift feeling of being suddenly without his father and mother, and the weight of Latchetts on his shoulders. It was too much for him and he was so unhappy that he—took a way out. (p. 17)

Alec Loding, Nancy's ne'er-do-well brother, will be invited to

Simon's coming-of-age festivities. Alec is the unpleasant, unattractive instigator of the crime. Bitterly resentful that his sister had not married into wealth and supported him, he resolves to get control of Simon's fortune. He discovers a man, Brat Farrar, who resembles Simon and consequently the missing Pat. Since Patrick's body was never discovered, the man could easily impersonate the missing son. At first, however, Brat Farrar wants nothing to do with Loding's scheme. Farrar had been a foundling, originally named Bart Farrell, and was raised in a orphanage with no idea of his family or background. The other children nicknamed him Brat and when he ran away to sea, the ship captain changed the last name to Farrar. Brat had travelled the world, going from one job to another. His only sense of belonging occurred when he worked with horses in America and that was ruined by an accident which left him lame. Finally, longing for a sense of permanence, he arrived in England.

Brat ponders the problem, tempted sorely by the horses at Latchetts. Like Grant and Lucy Pym, he has an "other side" with which he debates.

"It would be quite safe, you know," said a voice in him. "They wouldn't prosecute you even if they found out, because of the scandal. Loding said that."
    "Shut up," he said. "The thing's criminal." . . . .How would Loding be as a partner?
    "A very clever partner, believe me," said the voice.
    "A plain bad lot," he said. "I don't want any part of him." (p. 34)

By creating this dialogue, Tey enlivens and intensifies the argument with self. Again the scene could rapidly and easily be transposed to the stage. The "voice" of course wins the argument.

After Loding's coaching, Farrar calls on Mr. Sandal, the Ashby family solicitor. The solicitor at first mistakes him for Simon, but at length recognizes that Farrar is an Ashby.

"Yes? Do forgive me if I am a little confused. I didn't know that there were Ashby cousins."
    "There aren't. as far as I know."
    "No? Then—forgive me—which Ashby are you?"
    "Patrick."

Mr. Sandal's neat mouth opened and shut like a goldfish's. (p. 37) Claiming he had run away instead of committing suicide, Farrar carefully answers the man's questions. Basically, he tells the true story of his life, changing only the points Loding suggested. The solicitor is nearly convinced. Brat himself is elated.

Mr. Sandal calls Bee and informs her of the possible existence of Patrick. Bee who can scarcely remember what Pat looked like is upset and confused. Yet she wishes to believe it is the missing boy, perhaps to alleviate her own guilt feelings about his death.

Once again there is both preparation and foreshadowing as Kevin Macdermott (who later appears in *The Franchise Affair*), a friend of Sandal's, insists:

. . .It was too sensible. Too pat. Everything, Kevin said, was too pat for his liking. He said a boy coming home after years away would go home. (p. 51)

The terminology is also ironic. The reader suspects the complete treachery of Loding when the fate of the dentist who could have identified Pat is revealed.

"Well, now that poor old Hammond is to be no help to us—they never found him, did you know? Everything was just blown to dust." (p. 51)

Sandal suggests a surprise visit to Brat, and Bee is puzzled and a little frightened. The man indeed resembles Simon, but acts so very differently. They speak of horses and "She began to hope very strenuously that this was Patrick" (p. 56). As Bee leaves, she kisses Brat and says "Welcome back, my dear" (p. 58).

Bee postpones Simon's birthday celebration, using as an excuse Great Uncle Charles's delayed homecoming from the East. Finally, after tedious investigation, Mr. Sandal prounces Brat the missing Patrick. Informing the family is Aunt Bee's prerogative and she is shocked at Simon's reaction. "The shrunk white face with the blazing eyes had no resemblance to the Simon she knew" (p. 62). He vehemently insists "I don't believe for one moment that it is Patrick" (p. 63). The girls however, are both interested and excited.

Bee, unable to reconcile herself to Simon's negative behavior, calls on George Peck, the vicar. He explains that Simon is jealous and does not want to be deprived of Latchetts. Furthermore: "To Simon he is a remembered emotion; not a present one. He has no present love to fight his present—hatred with" (p. 69). The vicar himself could never comprehend Patrick's suicide, suggesting that, if Patrick is dead, he was murdered. Vicars, elderly aunts, and young children in the English mystery tradition are invariably innocent and suprisingly adroit in their perceptions.

Bee recognizes a certain lack of feeling in Simon which does not exist in Pat/Brat. She also recalls a sensitivity in Pat, a "great sense of obligation" (p. 74). Meanwhile, Brat, as if he were emotionally identical to Patrick, experiences both panic and guilt about the fraud. Nonetheless, showing some strength of character—or greed, depending on the point of view, he remains.

On Tuesday, Eleanor is sent to the station for Brat. Bee is unsure of Simon's reactions, expecting the worst. Eleanor, however, is very matter-of-fact and friendly. Ruth jumps out of the bushes as they turn into the drive and insists on riding to the house. There Jane rides up on her horse, and Brat manages to befriend the animal, if not the girl. Simon arrives just before lunch and surprisingly agrees that Brat is his brother.

He stood for a moment searching Brat's face; and his own was suddenly slack with relief.
"They won't have told you?" he said, drawling a little, "but I was prepared to deny with my last breath that you were Patrick. Now that I've seen you I take all that back. Of course you are Patrick." (p. 90)

Brat is puzzled by Simon's relief and slightly nervous about Jane's obvious resentment. Nonetheless, he is generally pleased to be at Latchetts. A reporter calls and insists on sending the story to a large London newspaper, much to Bee's horror.

Simon takes Brat to his room to give him some riding clothes and reveals through questioning that he does not believe the man to be Patrick. Brat is both excited and challenged by the game of "beating" Simon. With Aunt Bee, they go to the stables. Simon discusses the horses and treats Brat like another visitor. He suggests that Brat ride Timber, his horse, around the country-side. Brat is delighted with both horse and farm. As he stands on a hillside, he is surprised by a girl who mistakes him for Simon.

She confesses she is trying to have an affair with Simon, but so far has had little success. On the way back to the stables, Timber tries to brush off his rider. Brat senses that the horse is both difficult and possibly a killer, a fact that Eleanor later confirms. Interestingly, Simon had failed to mention the matter or warn Brat. Again the reader is permitted a quick glimpse of Simon's unpleasant and dangerous personality, foreshadowing his later murderous attempt on Brat's life.

Nancy and George Peck join the Ashbys for dinner. Everyone seems good-humored and even Eleanor dresses up for the occasion. Brat is wary of the vicar since he was Patrick's tutor, but Loding, the vicar's brother-in-law, had schooled Brat well. Everyone retires early. Bee and Eleanor privately discuss Brat, expressing ambivalent feelings of doubt and confidence in him.

On Wednesday, Brat and Bee visit the three tenant farms. Alec had primed him well for the farmers he met. As they travel between the farms, Bee plans the quiet birthday party for the boys. Mr. Sandal, of course, will be there with the papers to sign for Patrick's inheritance. Arriving at the Gates farm, Bee is delighted by a new horse the tenant has purchased for his daughter. Simon, however, when told of the horse, becomes furious. The horse is a winner, and Simon, who was attracted to the girl, finds her entry as a rival in an upcoming race unforgivable. Brat wonders "But what kind of heel was Simon that he could not love a rival?" (p. 150). Obviously, since he could not endure the rivalry of a girl he supposedly loved, the rivalry of a more likable brother would be impossible to bear. Once again Tey prompts the reader to wonder over Patrick's fate. Brat adds, "Patrick would not have gone sick with rage because his best girl had a better horse than he had. Patrick was all right" (p. 152). And later that evening he begins to wonder "where was Simon when Patrick went over the cliff?" (p. 154).

Thursday morning Brat and Bee go into nearby Westover. Bee shops for Mr. Sandal's dinner, and Brat goes in search of Macallan, the reporter who covered his return home. He asks the man to find Patrick's obituary in the back files of the paper. Brat learns that Patrick was first missed at dinner time, but no alarm was raised, it being assumed he'd wandered too far in his bird watching. By dark, however, phone calls were made and finally a search party established. At dawn Patrick's jacket was discovered by the cliffs with a note in the pocket. Albert Potticary, who discovered the body in *A Shilling for Candles,* found the jacket. Patrick's body was never found. The last person to see the boy was Abel Tusk, a shepherd who insisted the boy looked much as usual. Bee identified the note as in Patrick's handwriting.

Patrick had a very individual way of making his capital letters. And he was the only person I know who wrote with a stylograph.
She explained the nature of a stylograph. The one Patrick owned had been black vulcanite with a thin yellow spiral down the barrel. Yes, it was missing. He carried it always with him; it was one of his pet possessions. (p. 161)

Friday Brat finds a stack of presents by his breakfast plate and is both embarrassed and uncomfortable. After breakfast and opening the presents, Sandal explains "the whole economic history of Latchetts" (p. 166). Brat wishes to give Simon something, and finally Mr. Sandal agrees that a loan to get established elsewhere might not be out of place. Finally, the papers are signed and Brat is legally responsible for fraud.
Becoming more and more curious about Patrick's disappearance, Brat walks to the cliffs where the boy disappeared and meets old Abel the shepherd. He believes that Pat was never one to give in easily and was very surprised when the boy supposedly committed suicide. After resting, Brat goes to visit the blacksmith, Mr. Pilbean. He learns that Simon had frequented the forge the summer of the death and had made a sheep crook. By now, of course, the reader is far ahead of the detective and knows exactly the purpose of the sheep crook. The blacksmith, however, insists Simon was at the forge all day.
On Sunday the Ashbys go to church. Eleanor helps Brat through the social hurdles after the service. On Monday Brat goes to London to get clothes and settle business matters. He sends a "fat wad" of notes to Loding but "This first payment to his partner in crime left a taste in his mouth that was not entirely due to the gum on the envelope that he had licked" (p. 179).
At lunch Brat asks what Simon was doing while his twin was bird watching. Bee doesn't know and adds:

Simon changed after you went. I don't know whether it was the shock of your going or the lack of your sober companionship, but he was a different person afterwards. (p. 161)

As the days pass, Brat and Eleanor become close. Brat spends much of his spare time studying stud books and working in the stables. The stable hands now seem to prefer him to Simon. Bee writes to Uncle Charles, who will later become the *deus ex machina* of the novel, and explains what Patrick is like. Once again she sounds her favorite theme:

George Peck seems pleased with him, but I think finds it hard to forgive his silence all those years. I do too, of course. I find it inexplicable. One can only try to understand the immensity of the upheaval that sent him away from us. (p. 184)

Simon, distracted lately, often forgets to exercise his horse, Timber, and Brat does it for him. He enjoys it immensely, seeing Timber as "challenge, and excitement and satisfaction; Timber was question and glory" (p. 185). On one of his jaunts he meets again the girl who was trying to have an affair with Simon. It seems that he has now become "matey" with her and they meet often at a town pub. Brat wonders

Was it a sort of "larning" his family for the disappointment he had been caused? A sort of you-don't-like-me-therefore-I'll-take-up-with-Sheila-Parslow? A sorry-when-I'm-dead reaction? There was a very childish side to Simon. (p. 190)

When Simon realizes Brat has been exercising Timber, he is furious. Brat, correctly paranoiac, thinks that, if Simon continues to lose control, he might "show his hand and he would find out what Simon's plans for him were" (p. 194). Yet, the following morning, Simon apologizes.

The family go to Bures for the horse show and plan to stay the night. Brat is not looking forward to rooming with Simon, but he is excited about being near Eleanor. They drive down together and to Brat, each moment is precious. Tey's description of the horse show and the accompanying fair is accurate, colorful, and memorable, obviously based on personal, firsthand observation.

The contests go well for the Ashbys as Jane, Simon, and Bee win trophies. Brat chooses not to enter the competition and watches the exhibitions with interest. He feels uncomfortably jealous when he notices Eleanor speaking with an attractive man.

Simon is pitted against his former girlfriend, Peggy, in one of the contests. "No one, *no one*, was going to come between Simon

Ashby and the sun and get away with it" (p. 211). Yet he exhibits
great self-control in the ride. Brat notices a different side of
Simon as he works with his horse and, for a moment, almost likes
him. Generally, Tey's criminals are not *completely* without
redeeming qualities. Beau Nash is pleasant and likable, while
Mrs. Wallis is a kindly, protective mother. Simon, of course, is
particularly good with horses, a quality Tey admired greatly.

Later, Brat is persuaded to take part in the big race. As he is
walking Chevron, his horse, Simon reminds him to sign in and
offers to hold the horse while he does so. When Brat returns,
Simon is gone. He automatically checks the horse's gear and
discovers that the girth has loosened. It would have meant a bad
fall or worse if it had gone unnoticed. It gives Brat great pleasure
to win this last race of the day.

At the dance that evening, Brat happily spends his time with
Eleanor. As they eat, Eleanor suddenly looks at Brat.

"You're *not* my brother!" she said. "I couldn't feel the way I—" she
stopped, horrified.

She runs sobbing to her room. At the bar, Brat meets Simon who
is both ill-tempered and drunk. He states definitely that Brat is
not the missing Patrick.

There was a long silence while Brat searched the shining eyes with
their odd dark rim.
   "You killed him," he said, suddenly sure of it.
   "Of course I did." He leaned forward and looked delightedly at Brat.
"But you'll never be able to say so, will you?" (p. 222)

Brat asks him his motive.

"He was a very stupid little boy," he said in his airy "Simon" tone, "and
not worthy of Latchetts." Then he added, without facade: "I hated
him, if you want to know." (p. 222)

Simon further admits he will kill Brat if given half a chance. Brat,
caught in a dilemma, cannot betray this murderer because he
himself is guilty of fraud. Like Grant, Brat is shocked when his
worst fears are articulated by someone else. He knows he cannot
tolerate this "unholy alliance." But like so many other Tey

characters, he cannot decide upon a course of action and is temporarily, at least, immobilized.

On Thursday, Brat again goes to town to read about Patrick's inquest. He learns nothing. Returning to Latchetts, he rides out to a nearby hilltop to think. Suddenly he knows how Simon had murdered his brother and why he had been afraid that, by some miracle, it was the real Patrick who had returned. Like Miss Pym, however, he fears the consequences of his knowledge on the others. And so like Grant, the reader is not immediately aware of the detective's reasoning process. Searching for a solution, Brat resolves to visit the vicar, George Peck. The vicar, although aware of Brat's impersonation, is shocked to hear that Simon murdered his brother. Nonetheless, he insists that "if murder had been done, then the law must be invoked" (p. 235). While the vicar cannot believe Simon guilty, Brat is more concerned with the effect of his crime on the family.

The following day Simon, Eleanor, and Brat go into town to get their trophy cups engraved. Brat leaves them and buys some strong rope, determined somehow to get evidence against Simon. Late that night, after everyone is asleep, he takes the rope and goes to the old quarry. As he begins lowering himself into the pit, Simon appears and threatens to cut the rope.

"Cutting the rope won't do much good," he [Brat] said. "I'll only land in the branches of some tree farther down and yell my head off until someone comes."
   "I know better than that. A personal acquaintance of mine, this quarry is. Almost a relation, one might say." He expelled his breath in a whispered laugh. "A sheer drop to the ground, half a hillside away." (p. 242)

Brat eases himself up until he is almost back on the turf. Simon steps on his hand and tries to push him back over the ledge. Frantically, Brat grabs Simon's foot. As Tey humorously remarks, "It is very upsetting to have one's foot grasped from below when one is standing on the very edge of a precipice" (p. 242). Simon tries desperately to stab Brat.

   "Drop that knife!" he said.
   As he said it he felt the turf at the quarry edge settle a little and slide forward. It made no difference to him, except to press him out a little

from the face of the cliff. But to Simon, already bent over by the weight of Brat's arms and body, it was fatal. (p. 243)

Simon knocks Brat off the cliff in his fall, and they both tumble down the cliff.

Two days later, Bee waits in a café across from the hospital for news. The doctor says that "his" condition remains the same. Until the arrival of George Peck, the reader is not aware which of the men Bee is waiting for. The vicar tells her, "I have come to bring you comfort that Simon is dead" (p. 245). He has with him Patrick's distinctive stylograph found near some bones at the quarry bottom. Bee, however, is more concerned with Brat, insisting that they must know his true identity. The family has taken the news of their brother's death well, and Eleanor is delighted that Brat was not her brother. A hospital aid arrives and asks Bee to return at once. Brat has regained consciousness and asks for her. She reassures him that she is not angry and that he will ride again.

On Wednesday the *deus ex machina* arrives in the form of Uncle Charles.

Charles took one look at the young face with the slack jaw, the blue shadows under the closed eyes, and the grey haze of stubble, and said: " Walter."
. . . ."That is exactly what Walter used to look like, at his age, when he had a hangover." (p. 249)

The police, vicar, and family conspire to cover up the entire matter. The verdict of the coroner's court was death by misadventure for Simon. Brat is identified as the son of Walter and a nurse named Mary Woodward. Bee resolves to take Brat away to convalesce, and Eleanor resolves to marry him, so his future is settled. Uncle Charles will direct Latchetts and the girls.

II *The Critics*

Brat Farrar was well liked by the critics as well as readers. Ralph Partridge in the *New Statesman & Nation* comments: ". . . Miss Tey has a wonderful gift for portraying impostors; and the character of Brat Farrar combining charm with deceit, is a triumph of her art."[2] The critic for the *New Yorker* insists: "Her book is the best of its kind in many months."[3] Anthony Boucher, one of the most noted critics in fiction genre, finds Brat's dilemma fascinating, and adds that "the ingenious plot is warmly and suspensefully unfolded."[4]

III   *The Character of Brat*

The critics' praise was well placed. Tey for the first time uses a character who is openly unsure of his identity. While Christine Clay, Grant, and even Lucy Pym were unsure of themselves, they competently hid their problem. Brat, however, lacks both name and identity. He is the equivalent of the unknown corpse in Tey's earlier novels and of Tisdall, the suspect in *A Shilling for Candles*, whose name was changed.

Brat sees himself as manipulated by powers beyond his control, by fate. It is interesting that these "powers" are all personified father figures—the father who left him, the captain who took him on board ship, Alec who coached him, Sandal who accepted him, the vicar who stimulated him to accidental murder, and finally Uncle Charles who gives him his identity. Once his true self is settled, however, a drastic change occurs and it seems as though his life will be directed by mother figures, Aunt Bee and Eleanor. He has at last found someone other than a horse to love and to love him in return. A limp traditionally suggests an emotional as well as a physical cripple, and Brat's injured leg is symbolic of his inability to love. Aunt Bee's constant reassurance that "it can be fixed" is true both physically as well as emotionally. Brat's identity is ultimately "fixed" also. The horses, the overriding symbol in the novel, finally help establish this identity, as well as suggesting something admirable, trainable, yet basically unpredictable and wily. Timber, of course, is the animal double of Simon, as Brat himself points out.

IV   *Repeated Motifs*

Once again as in *Miss Pym Disposes*, Tey has characters die as the result of a fall. In *Miss Pym* the fall was from gym equipment; here the murderer falls to his death in the quarry to lie beside his victim. Both Patrick and Simon lose their identities and their lives when they fall into the deep pit. Ironically, Brat discovers his identity as a direct result of the fall.

V *Patterns of Doubling*

In *Brat Farrar,* Tey uses an elaborate system of doubling. Her previous work dealing with doubles, *Expensive Halo,* was inexpert and clumsy, but apparently excellent practice. The doubles in *Brat Farrar* are carefully balanced and articulated. The "other sides" that argue with Inspector Grant and Lucy Pym are in this novel personified as real characters. Farrar argues with his criminally inclined "voice" only to discover it personified in the nearly identical murderer, Simon. Each character in the novel has a double, that is, someone like him in position (and in three instances physically identical) but usually opposite in character. The double can be either an angel or a tempting devil, but it nevertheless represents instinctual, albeit unconscious, drives that are present in the physical double. Simon, for example, can be kind and patient while Brat surely has murderous desires like Simon. It is as if each individual were placed before a mirror that reflects the opposite of what is before it.

Most obviously are the twins opposites. Patrick, kind, gentle, and considerate, is opposed to Simon, who is cruel, selfish, and egotistical. They clash physically, and Patrick is dead. Even Aunt Bee distrusts and doubts Simon to some extent. Brat, too, senses something unpleasant about Simon and is "repelled" by him. Yet no character is ever all good or all bad. Simon, in spite of his negative behavior regarding Brat, can be quite charming. And he is superbly patient and understanding with horses.

Alec Loding is, in some respects, Brat's double. The instigator of the action, he is selfish, greedy, and unprincipled. He, like Brat and Simon, is criminally inclined, though careful not to be implicated. Brat does protect Alec's identity even when his own is discovered.

Brat, the third Ashby, bears a physical resemblance to Patrick, yet synthesizes traits of both brothers. He is gentle and considerate, sensitive and understanding. For example, he can quite accurately sense the feelings of Jane when she apologizes for her behavior. Nonetheless, he determinedly sets out to steal Latchetts from its rightful owner through lies and deception. His only punishment is the temporary loss of Latchetts, to be regained, the reader can assume, when he marries Eleanor.

Ironically, Brat and Simon both commit murder, although in

Brat's case it is "accidental." Neither man is directly punished for this crime either. Simon's death occurs only when he is attempting a second murder, and Brat is excused by a verdict of death by misadventure.

Brat illustrates once again the agony and the ecstasy of Tey's central characters. He knows his illegal and immoral position and exults in it, although he is burdened with pangs of conscience. These he stays by becoming the dead boy's "champion." Like Grant, however, he continually questions both his motives and feelings.

. . . and his thoughts, running on approval and disapproval, went to Bee. What was it that he had felt when Bee took his hand to lead him to the interview this afternoon? . . . Why the surge of warmth under his heart, and what kind of emotion was it anyway? (p. 138)

Brat does not make decisions easily and is greatly relieved when "fate" once again steps in and Simon is neatly tossed into the quarry. Brat is then relieved of any obligation to reveal Simon's perfidy.

VI   *The Double Ingenue*

Jane and Ruth, physical twins, resemble the two aspects of Tey's beloved ingenue seen in both *A Shilling for Candles* and *Miss Pym Disposes.* Jane. the determined, casual, sensible, ragamuffin is similar to Erica, the chief constable's daughter in *A Shilling for Candles.* Jane's old white pony on which she tours the countryside is surely the equivalent of Erica's old car, " Tinny."

Ruth, Jane's double, is the mirror opposite to her. Her flair for the dramatic, interest in clothing, and ability always to remain neat and fresh are the complete opposite of Jane's personality. If Ruth seems familiar to the reader, it is because she "is" Teresa Desterro, the Nut Tart of *Miss Pym Disposes,* without the South American accent. It is almost as if Tey were using a stock company with the same actors playing different but similar parts in each novel.

All Tey's ingenues are sensitive, full of insight, amusing, and precocious.

"If I ran away for years and years, would you believe I was me, Jane?" Ruth asked.

"You wouldn't stay away for years and years, anyhow," Jane said.
"What makes you think I wouldn't?"
"You'd come home in no time at all."
"Why would I come home?"
"To see how everyone was taking your running away." (p. 64-65)

Finally, there is little ambivalence in these characters; that is, they are exactly what they appear to be; no confusion or complications exist in the characters. It is if the author were saying, "This type, this girl, is one of the few reliable persons in my world. She will never deceive me." A dramatic change takes place, however, when Tey writes *The Franchise Affair*.

VII   *The Aunt Mothers*

Aunt Bee, another incarnation of Miss Pym, is understanding and motherly. Physically, she has "a face like a very expensive cat" (p. 12). "The long-necked, short-haired kind that show their small chins. Heraldic cats" (p. 12). Tey's aunts or aunt-like characters are not beautiful, but can look attractive at least on occasion. They are also prone to deep guilt feelings, Bee because of Patrick's death and Lucy because of her actions regarding Innes. Both have contradictory and irreconcilable emotions which they indicate openly.

Seven-eights of her wanted Patrick back; warm, and alive, and dear; wanted it passionately. The other eighth shrank from the upheaval of the happy Ashby world that his return would bring with it. When she caught this renegade eighth at its work she reproved it and was suitably ashamed of herself; but she could not destroy it. (p. 60)

Bee's double is the vicar's wife, Nancy Peck. Physically, Nancy is the opposite of Bee, beautiful and even famous. Nonetheless, she serves in the motherly role of understanding confidant who specializes in soothing troubled brows. She, like Bee, is sensitive, but she keeps her emotions hidden, presenting only a cool and beautiful exterior.

VIII   *The Father Uncle*

Since aside from her first novel, no real mother or father characters exist in Tey's novels, Aunt Bee and Nancy must assume mother-roles. Likewise, the vicar and Uncle Charles assume father roles. Whereas Aunt Bee is insecure, doubtful of her abilities as a mother, and guilt-ridden, the father figures act as though from an Olympian station. They deal unemotionally and rationally with the problems engendered by the children. The vicar and Uncle Charles appear as if by magic at critical moments. The vicar insists that justice be placed before love, unlike the decisions of a mother-figure who would inevitably place love before justice. And through his advice, George Peck goads Brat into the action that kills the evil brother. Uncle Charles appears when Brat, injured in the struggle with Simon, is near death. Immediately he identifies him as his ne'er-do-well brother Walter's son, thus giving Brat instant identity, a past as well as a future. His identification prepares the way for Bee's adoption of Brat as well as Eleanor's marriage with him. Fathers, it seems, straighten out matters bungled by mother and children.

IX *Double Doubles*

Simon and Brat are doubles of the twin ingenues, Jane and Ruth. The girls, like their brothers, have their own interests and identities and are opposites in dress and personality. They are all bright and competent, nonetheless. However, while Simon and Brat are both to some extent criminal and unprincipled, the girls are the opposite. And while both males are jealous of each other, the girls take pride in each other's accomplishments. They reveal none of the bitter rivalry of Simon and Brat.

X *The Love Interests*

Eleanor has in effect two doubles, Sheilah and Peggy. Eleanor is attracted to Brat while the other girls are attracted to Simon. All the girls seem initially detached, as if their interest were curious and not emotional. Yet each goes out of her way to meet her man. Only in the closing chapters do both Eleanor and Peggy reveal sensitivity and emotion as both weep because their chosen male appears unavailable. In Peggy's case, the barrier is Simon's pride, while Eleanor is stymied by Brat's initial lie. Only Eleanor's hopes have the possibility of fulfillment.

XI   *The Murder, the Victim, the Clue*

Once again, as in *A Shilling for Candles,* a death by drowning occurs before the action begins. Then too, what appears at first as accident or suicide is in fact murder. In *A Shilling for Candles, Miss Pym Disposes,* and *Brat Farrar,* the murders are staged as accidents and· can be assumed as such except for some unintentional clue left by the murder—the button, the rosette, or the pencil. In Tey's final novel, *The Singing Sands,* the murder is also staged as an accident, but in this case the victim leaves a clue that eventually leads to the truth. The clues are of the same type, common physical objects used by the murderer or his victim with regularity.

Again, the victim scarcely exists. Patrick is abstract to the point of extinction. Simon, however, the second victim, is like Rouse in *Miss Pym Disposes.* Having committed a crime (for Rouse cheating, for Simon murder) the criminal dies an "accidental death." The perpetrator of 'this final crime is scarcely punished. We are to assume, one supposes, that the initial crime is the more serious.

XII   *In Place of Another*

The theme in *Brat Farrar* is the familiar "in place of another." Brat initially takes the place of Alec after being carefully coached in the act of criminal fraud. (Alec ironically creates a Frankenstein in Brat who assumes the identity of an Ashby so perfectly that he becomes one.) Brat then takes the place of the dead Patrick and becomes his champion. Finally, as the result of Simon's "accidental" death, he replaces Simon in the family's affections. Simon, in fact, dies in place of Brat, Bee replaces the mother, and Uncle Charles replaces Brat's wandering father, Walter. Finally, even Timber, the unpredictable horse, replaces Brat's beloved Smokey, the horse left in America. The ends are all tied up artistically and economically.

CHAPTER 8

The Franchise Affair

*T*HE *Franchise Affair* (1949) indicates a departure from Tey's previous approach to detective fiction. Here she deals with a historical theme, the infamous Elizabeth Canning story, but places it in a modern setting. This is the first of her two novels dealing with a historical mystery.

I   *The Plot*

Like *A Shilling for Candles* (1936), the opening chapter in *The Franchise Affair* presents a serene, dependable, and perhaps even dull world. The town of Milford is typical of hundreds of others with its gossip, clashes between old and new, and its complete predictability. Trouble begins, as in a melodrama, with the ringing of the phone in the office of Robert Blair, Hayward, and Bennett. Marion Sharpe, owner and resident of The Franchise, a run-down old house on Larborough Road, quickly explains: "I'm supposed to have kidnapped someone. Or abducted them, or something. I can't explain over the telephone. And anyhow I need someone now." Although Blair tries to put her off, she insists, "I don't want a criminal lawyer. I want a friend" (p. 22).

The Franchise is an ugly house, isolated in the country—a perfect setting for a criminal kidnapping. When Blair arrives, Inspector Grant of Scotland Yard has preceded him. Marion is accused of having kidnapped and beaten a girl named Elizabeth Kane who had been missing from the home of her guardians for a month. She had been staying with an aunt nearby prior to her disappearance.

The police took all the usual measures but before they could really get going the girl turned up. She walked into her home near Aylesbury late

113

one night wearing only a dress and shoes, and in a state of complete exhaustion. (p. 18)

The girl was only fifteen years old, and her story was deceptively simple. She had been waiting for the bus to return home when two women stopped their car to offer her a ride. Since she apparently had missed the bus, she accepted. They took her to their home where they drugged and imprisoned her. Later when she refused to act as their servant, they beat her. The girl identifies Marion and her mother as the two women and accurately describes The Franchise and the attic in which she was supposedly imprisoned.

When the police and their witness leave, Marion insists that the girl is both a liar and oversexed. She is, as it turns out, absolutely correct. Marion is a type of character not seen at length in Tey's previous books—a bright, outspoken, intuitive woman who, against all odds, is at peace with herself. It is as if the clever ingenue had at last grown up.

More than a week later, Inspector Hallams visits Blair at his office. No proceedings would be taken, he states, though the Yard was not dropping the case. They failed to find the truck driver who supposedly picked up the girl after her escape. Robert happy with the news, sends his cousin Nevil with a note to Marion. Nevil is at once entranced with her, and she in turn finds him amusing, much to Blair's secret disgust. He himself is also developing an interest in this unusual woman.

It seems as if the case will die down, but on Friday, a sensational newspaper, the *Ack-Emma*, blasts the news of the "Franchise Affair" all over England. A picture of the wronged girl is on the front page. It is interesting to note that most people who saw Kane's picture admit that her "type" is usually a most inventive liar and probably something of a tramp. "'Where do you think the girl was, then, all the time?' '. . . . I'd say definitely—oh, but definitely—on, the tiles,' Stanley said, and went out to attend to a customer" (p. 58). Nonetheless, many people apparently do believe her story. This ambivalent attitude toward a questionable young person was also seen in *Miss Pym Disposes* in Lucy's feelings toward Rouse and in *Brat Farrar* with Aunt Bee's attitude toward Simon. Tey, at least, seems to find both character and attitude typical of English life.

Blair is extremely disturbed by the *Ack-Emma* publication, as are the police. There is, however, little that can be done since "We have a fine free press" (p. 59). The suggestion is that a free press is not altogether a good idea since it causes pain to innocent people and inevitably hampers the police in their work.

The lawyer decides to approach the case from the opposite viewpoint of the police. Instead of proving Kane's story true, he sets out to prove it false, to discover her real whereabouts during those four weeks. He goes first to visit the foster parents. He learns that Leslie, their son, was devoted to the girl until he became engaged several months previously. He also learns that her bruises looked more as if she had been knocked about than whipped. This, again, is exactly what happened. Finally and most important, he learns that she has a photographic memory and has been pampered and adored and spoiled.

Even playing dolls' tea-parties, she would never imagine the things on the plates as most children are quite happy to do. There had to be a real thing there, even if it was only a little cube of bread. Usually it was something nicer, of course; it was a good way to wangle an extra and she was always a little greedy. (p. 71)

More indicative of Betty's character are the comments of her foster mother about the child's attitude when she first arrived. "She cried because she didn't like the food. I don't remember her ever crying for her mother" (p. 72). Mrs. Wynn, the foster mother, is somewhat puzzled by the fact that Betty had a golden lipstick in her pocket when she returned, but she will not admit her puzzlement or perhaps her fear. Robert then visits the bombed-out neighborhood in which the Kanes had lived before shipping their child to the country. Here they were killed. Mrs. Kane, he learns, had often gone partying and dancing, but seldom with her husband. "But she was a bad mother and a bad wife, that's flat and no one ever said anything to the contrary" (p. 79). This will later be used to prove that old saw, "like mother, like daughter." Furthermore, Tey suggests the dangers of adoption— a conservative but not unusual view.

While in London, Robert visits a lawyer friend, Kevin McDermott. "And as a well-known defending counsel his knowledge of human nature was extensive, varied, and peculiar" (p. 76). They both agree as to the logical and probable aspects of the girl's story. Nonetheless, McDermott insists it is "A complete

invention from beginning to end" (p. 86). This he knows intuitively, it appears.

Scotland Yard, meanwhile, has problems, and here begins the
animosity and hostility toward Kane that is reiterated throughout
the book.

All Scotland Yard's energies were devoted to proving the Sharpes
guilty and Betty Kane's story true for the very good reason that they
believed the Sharpes to be guilty. But what each one of them ached in
his private soul to do was to push Betty Kane down the *Ack-Emma's*
throat; and they could only do that by proving her story nonsense. (pp.
87–88)

At Betty's aunt's, Blair discovers that the girl spent much of her
time in the nearby town of Larborough at the cinema or bus
riding. He quickly ascertains that a double decker bus had been
on the Milford route during the girl's stay. She could easily have
seen the yard of The Franchise from the top deck.

At The Franchise, meanwhile, townspeople have been gawk-
ing and threatening, and Nevil has stood by to protect the
Sharpes. Irritated that Nevil seems so much a part of the Sharpe
household, Robert vows to pursue the case and discover the man,
Mr. X, whom he assumes the girl was meeting. The lawyer goes
to coffee shops trying to find a waitress who would remember
Kane. Finally, by accident, a waiter at the Midland Hotel brings
up the subject and recognizes her. She came often and "picked
up" a man on one occasion and never returned. Elated because
there is some proof of his theory, Blair is nonetheless down-
hearted since he has come to the end of his resources. He feels
that there is little else he can do. He obtains a list of hotel
residents at the time and returns home.

Back at The Franchise, someone painted the word "Fascists"
on the wall. The tranquil English town is turning into an angry
mob. Later that evening as Stanley and Bill, owners of Blair's
garage, paint over the word, more mobs appear and break all the
downstairs windows of the house, injuring Stanley. Nonetheless,
the women refuse to move, and Stanley offers to stay on as a
boarder and protect them.

The lawyer now has become very pleased with his situation—a
balloon the author enjoys puncturing.

He was on calling terms with Scotland Yard; he was agent for a pair of scandalous women; he had become an amateur sleuth; and he had been witness of mob violence. His whole world looked different. Even the people he met looked different. (p. 131)

When he arrives home, however, he discovers another complication in the Franchise Affair. The father of Nevil's fiancé has decided to champion Betty Kane. Unfortunately, he is a bishop known for his liberal attitudes. In desperation, Blair hires an inquiry agent to help track down Kane's whereabouts.

On Friday the bishop's letter appears and though it pleases neither Blair nor Grant, it is not as bitter and outspoken as it might have been.

Blair relaxes again, enjoying the fact that he is "not part of the landscape any more, after all those years of comfortable merging" (p. 147). The reader is now fully prepared for the peripety or reversal in fortune for the main characters. The novel, in fact, carefully follows the outline of a well-made play. As in the well-made play invented by Alexandre Dumas *fils* and perfected by Eugene Scribe, *The Franchise Affair* is ingeniously written and contains a cautionary thesis. Everything that sustains suspense and delays the resolution dominates everything else. At the basis of the novel, like the *pièce bien fait,* is a secret known to the reader—Kane's guilty lies—but withheld from nearly everyone else until she is unmasked in a climactic scene. That her fraudulence is illuminated in a courtroom scene is also "well made." While *The Franchise Affair* follows the demands of common sense, the final resolution carries with it a moral judgment.

As a reversal, Grant appears with an arrest warrant for the Sharpes. He has found two corroborative witnesses. One person saw the girl picked up by a car resembling the Sharpes'. Secondly, the girl who used to help out at The Franchise states that she heard screams from the attic during the period that Kane was missing. Furthermore, she mentioned this to a friend, Gladys Rees, who corroborates her story. Blair persuades Grant to issue a summons instead, but the Inspector seems angry with the Sharpes. Hallam comments:

Well it's my belief—strictly between ourselves—that he can't forgive them for fooling them. . . . He's famous at the Yard for his good judgment of people, you see; and, again between ourselves, he didn't much care for the Kane girl or her story; and he liked them even less when he had seen the Franchise people, in spite of all the evidence. Now he thinks the wool was pulled over his eyes, and he's not taking it lightly. (p. 161)

When the summons is delivered, Marion insists that Rose Glyn, the girl who used to help, had been fired for stealing her watch. She adds bitterly, speaking of Kane: "I could kill that girl; I could kill her. My God, I could torture her twice a day for a year, and then begin again on New Year's Day" (p. 166). Again and again the note of bitter hostility if not hatred is sounded. Possibly the author had developed a deep dislike for innocent-looking, but sexually overactive young girls. Blair adds:

To have been the heroine of a newspaper sensation, to say nothing of the adored centre of a loving and sympathetic family, and then to be uncovered to the public gaze as a liar, a cheat and a wanton? I think she would mind. And there is one thing she would mind particularly. One result of her escapade was that she got back Leslie Wynn's attention she had lost when he became engaged. As long as she is a wronged heroine she is assured of that attention; once we show her up she has lost it for good. (p. 167)

And again, he later insists "I'm going to undress her in public. . . . I'm going to strip her of every rag of pretence, in open court, so that everyone will see her for what she is" (p. 173). The following day McDermott and Blair visit the Sharpes for lunch. The reader discovers that Mrs. Sharpe's brother was a famous horse trainer and that she was once wealthy and knew all the "right" people. This, of course, wipes out any negative effects her odd behavior might have had. After lunch Marion points out an error in Kane's statement. She stated she could see all of the drive from the round attic window and this is not true. They decide to save this evidence for the Assizes and present no defense at the police court or preliminary hearing. During the wait for Assizes, the Sharpe case seems to go nowhere. This temporary frustration occurs in all Tey novels. The main character reaches a point where he seems unable to undertake any positive action. The only unusual event during this time occurs when Marion's watch arrives in the mail with a note. Blair assumes Rees sent it back and that she was being blackmailed into testifying by Glyn. Ramsden a private detective employed by Blair obtains a copy of the girl's handwriting, and it does indeed match the note.

Incapable of action, Blair, like Grant, becomes depressed and miserable. With the new evidence, his clients will probably get off, but Kane will not be publicly humiliated. Troubled and unhappy, he pours out his problems to his Aunt Lin who promises to pray for a miracle.

The miracle arrives the following morning when Mr. Lange, a hotelkeeper in Copenhagen, arrives and identifies the girl as a Mrs. Chadwick who spent the four weeks at his hotel with her husband. From here it is not difficult to track down Chadwick, a travelling salesman.

The night before the trial, when the Sharpes are in town, The Franchise is destroyed by fire. Stanley and Blair suspect arson, but cannot prove it.

Slowly the trial edges toward the fatal revelation. Chadwick admits Kane spent the time with him and later stayed at his cottage, and his wife admits she "knocked around" the little trollop. After the trial, Marion is more disturbed over Mrs. Wynn's terrible enlightenment about her daughter's character than she is about the destruction of The Franchise. Blair proposes marriage and Marion refuses, planning to stay with a cousin in Canada. The lawyer, unable to accept a dull life again, goes with her.

II *The Critics*

The Franchise Affair was well received by the critics. James Sandoe, well known for his incisive and penetrating criticism of detective fiction, states:

The mysteries in my library crowd the room in which I work, sprawl into the hallway and fill most of the basement. But if I had to reduce these unruly holdings to a single shelf, one book certain to be on that shelf is the "The Franchise Affair." Apart from its solid merits as a tale of detection it has the pungency and the vitality that is warm testimony of sound writing.[2]

Will Cuppy adds: "Recommended to all those nice people who keep hollering for something first class."[3]

III   *Tey's Style*

Undoubtedly *The Franchise Affair* is one of Tey's most polished and artistic works. The characters are carefully drawn with a penetrating insight that exposes both strengths and weaknesses. The action moves systematically through the traditional steps of problem, temporary success, and reversal to the climax in a grinding courtroom scene. Above all, the atmosphere is both memorable and frightening. Beginning in the quiet, orderly, and secure office of Robert Blair, it progresses through the increasing horrors of false accusations and mob violence to the terrible courtroom where a mother is stripped of her illusions as her daughter is stripped of her lies.

IV   *Tey's Sources*

In *The Franchise affair,* Tey reconstructs, modernizes, and fictionalizes the 1753 story of Elizabeth Canning. Possibly her source was the 1945 fictional recreation *Elizabeth is Missing* by Lillian de la Torre, or the Arthur Machen book *The Canning Wonder.* Whatever the source, the story aroused in Tey violent and angry emotion particularly aimed at the character of Betty Kane, the baby-faced, lying trollop.

Elizabeth Canning was "an infernal liar."[4] Betty Kane is guilty of the same sin. Canning's information about the house in which she was imprisoned was inconsistent and inaccurate like Kane's. Her description of the room was vague and general and often wrong in detail. She also incorrectly described the view from the window.

Elizabeth Canning came in a chaise; it is quite possible, nay, probable, that she looked out of the window as the chaise went very slowly on its way; it is possible and probable that she looked about her curiously enough when the chaise stopped before Mrs. Wells's house.[5]

So Betty Kane too described what she saw from the bus rather than the view from the window.

Like Betty Kane, Elizabeth Canning had been visiting her aunt and uncle. She was, however, abducted by two men rather than two women. She was taken initially to the kitchen of the house.

According to Machen, however, the two women there asked Elizabeth to be a prostitute, not a servant. When she refused, they took her clothing and imprisoned her. Elizabeth identified "a gipsy," Mary Squires, as the woman who detained her. Notice that the name of Marion Sharpe is not unsimilar to Mary Squires. The old woman who supposedly corroborated with Mary Squires was called "Mother" Wells. In the Tey version, the old woman is Marion's mother. Canning escaped after about a month and arrived home covered with bruises as did Betty Kane. In court, Canning's story was supported by another girl, a former lodger at Mother Wells's, not a servant like Rose Glyn. She too later retracted her tale. The townspeople, immediately assuming the guilt of the women, raised money to help the poor girl. Everyone, in fact, rallied to her defense. Machen speculates that Canning spent the missing time in a brothel, irritated the Madam, and was punished by imprisonment and starvation. Betty Kane spent her time living with a travelling salesman and was later beaten by his wife. Mrs. Canning, like Mrs. Wynn, lied to others and herself about her daughter's behavior and her clothing when she arrived home, insisting that the girl had worn a shift for three weeks and that it gave no evidence of debauchery.

"I said, there was one thing in her favor, she had not been debauched; I said: 'Reach the shift to this gentlewoman'; I said: 'Let her judge the case and see that your child has not been debauched': . . . 'Look over it well; do you think this has been worn three weeks and three days?' 'No,' says she . . . 'I don't think that is likely. . . .'" then Mrs. Canning said: 'Do you come here to set my other friends against me. . .'?"[6]

Yet, Mrs. Canning was "a fine, likely woman as any, and one who commanded respect."[7]

Tey's fictionalization of the Canning story simplifies it considerably. She eliminates the dubious male friends of Mrs. Canning as well as the score of witnesses corroborating both the "gipsy's" story and Canning's. Mary Squires was an amazingly ugly widow with several adult children who travelled with her. Marion Sharpe was attractive and single. Thus Tey could add the very low key love interest between Marion and the lawyer, Robert Blair.

V   *Symbolism of the Title*

In naming the Sharpes' house Franchise, Tey makes it a symbol for the action in the the novel. The word "franchise" comes originally from *franc,* meaning free. It suggests freedom from servitude or any other restriction. Presently the word has several meanings including suffrage. Marion and her mother are ultimately freed both from the house and the suspicions aroused by Kane. Marion, as stated previously, is an independent liberated woman, determined to make her own way in an indifferent not hostile world. Ironically, by entitling the novel *The Franchise Affair,* Tey describes the Sharpes' ultimate freedom and Kane's affair with the salesman.

VI   *Tey's Distancing*

The viewpoint in *The Franchise Affair* is, as in *Miss Pym Disposes,* not that of the police, but of a person intimately involved in the action, in this case, the lawyer Robert Blair. Unlike her contemporaries, Christie and Sayers, Tey illustrates her independence from her fictional detective in *The Franchise Affair,* as well as in *Miss Pym Disposes.* Inspector Grant plays a very minor role indeed, appearing first with Betty Kane when she views The Franchise and later with warrant in hand for the arrest of the Sharpes.

Again, as in *Miss Pym Disposes* and *The Man in the Queue,* there is very little real detective work resulting in the solution of the crime. In fact, there is no crime to speak of. Kane and others commit perjury and her idyll in Copenhagen was perhaps immoral, but there is no murder. The only violence is that exhibited by the faceless mob against The Franchise. Unlike other mystery authors, Tey is not enamored of murder. In *To Love and Be Wise* and *The Franchise Affair,* there is no death at all. In her other works, the murder either takes place before the novel begins or occurs in the first chapter. The one exception is *Miss Pym Disposes* where Rouse's accidental murder occurs near the climax of the work. In all of her writings, Tey maintains a distance between the narrator and unpleasantness so that even the mob attack is not as terrifying or frightful as it could be.

The answer to Kane's whereabouts is hinted at first by Mrs. Sharpe in chapter 2. "Is the girl a virgin? . . . If I had been missing for a month from my home it is the first thing that my mother would have wanted to know about me" (pp. 29–30).

But only through a series of "accidents" is the truth revealed. The hotel owner accidentally sees the picture of Kane and mentions it when he later visits England. Chadwick accidentally returns just in time for the trial. Gladys Rees, guilty in conscience, returns Marion's watch with a note "I don't want none of it" in her distinctive scrawl. Blair and Nevil, among others, guess at the truth about Kane quickly but are at a loss for solid evidence. Perhaps this is more in tune with a modern world of corrupt officials and lying civil servants where the truth can only be guessed at or accidentally revealed. There is none of the reassurance of the Holmes era where a superior detective could arrive at the truth through brilliant deductions and reveal all to a delightfully surprised reader in the final chapter.

VII   *Worlds Contrasted*

The author seems to enjoy this contrast in worlds since it appears often in her works. For example, Robert Blair's private world, like that of the town in which he lives, is initially staid, predictable, and dull, bounded by old ladies' wills on one side and a traditional tea tray on the other. Suddenly, with the ringing of the phone, he is plunged into the tortured lives of the Sharpes. Once again the author is stating that the world is a sort of Alice-in-Wonderland affair where all appearances are misleading and the world can slip alarmingly out of kilter. The Sharpes, supposedly wealthy, are not. The residents of Milford, supposedly placid country folk, become a sadistic mob very rapidly. Blair, the town lawyer, becomes an active participant in a criminal case and even to some extent a poet. Nevil, his cousin, a blazing liberal poet, becomes a conservative hard-working lawyer. Marion, who looks like "a gipsy" and seems remote and possibly cruel, is in fact sensitive and kind. She, like Innes in *Miss Pym Disposes,* is the real victim since she suffers from the selfishly motivated action of another. The most obvious example of false appearances is Betty Kane, who looks like an innocent school girl, but is in fact a slut and tramp. Nor, for that matter does anyone even live up to their own self-image. Marion is not as remote as she would like to appear, her mother not quite as "sharp," Robert, not quite as conservative, and Nevil not quite as liberal.

VIII *Character Types*

Surprisingly, in *The Franchise Affair* Tey abandons or radically alters most of her favorite character types. The witty ingenue is not present. Instead, old Mrs. Sharpe is the outspoken purveyor of wit and truth. Inspector Grant is relegated to a very minor role, and Blair assumes the role of searcher for truth. He suffers none of the terrible conscience pangs of Grant, his only regret being his hitherto dull life. Nonetheless, he does endure the setbacks and frustrations Grant often saw. The foolish young man—Lamont in *Man in the Queue,* Robert in *A Shilling for Candles,* and Edward in *Miss Pym Disposes*—is not directly involved in the crime, nor does he remain foolish for long. Nevil rapidly becomes involved in protecting the Sharpes. The "saving woman" like Miss Dinmont in *The Man in the Queue* does not appear. The criminal with enormous ego, pride, and lack of sensitivity does reappear. Kane is in many respects similar to Beau Nash—adored, doted on; her ego is monstrous. "But with an egotism like Betty Kane's there is no adjustment. She expects the world to adjust itself to her. The criminal always does. . . ." (p. 222). The clever, likable young ingenue has finally become a monster.

The often woolly-minded but lovable aunt figure appears in *The Franchise Affair* in Tey's original form. Aunt Lin seems foolish and superficial, but is actually kind and intuitive like Miss Pym and Aunt Bee. It is she who prays for miracles and gets them.

"The trouble with you, dear, is that you think of an angel of the lord as a creature with wings, whereas he is probably a scruffy little man in a bowler hat. Anyhow, I shall pray very hard this afternoon, and tonight too, of course; and by tomorrow perhaps help will be sent" (p. 214).

Finally and most important, Tey here fully develops the character of the unwomanly woman. First seen in Henrietta in *Miss Pym Disposes,* who chose apologetically to make school and students her family, the unwomanly woman is developed in *The Franchise Affair* into a truly significant character. Perhaps she could be termed a liberated woman, though no doubt that would be farthest from the author's mind. She is free from male domination (and always will be even if married), independent, and outspoken. Yet there is none of the crusader in Marion, nor is there the guilt we saw in Henrietta. She is her own person, aware of responsibilities, aware of her physical and emotional drawbacks, and sensing deeply the problem of others. She is truly free and self-content. And this character type *only once* reappears in any of Tey's following novels.

IX *The House As Symbol*

In retelling the Canning story, Tey increases its horror and mystery by setting it at The Franchise, a remote house with iron gates. The house itself suggests the isolation of both the Sharpes and Kane as well as the emptiness of Blair's life. Its small round window from which Kane insists she saw the driveway implies a limited view of truth and existence, the initial condition of all the characters except perhaps Kane. The symbolic burning points to the destruction of the old life and the cleansed beginning of a new outlook. All that was ugly and corrupt is destroyed. It neatly foreshadows McDermott's success in court.

X *Themes*

Two points are so consistently reiterated in the novel that they cannot be ignored. First, the reader is impressed by the tremendous animosity of the characters toward Kane. Marion, Blair, and Nevil reveal deep hatred reminiscent of *Othello*. "Why, we have galls; and though we have some grace, / yet have we some revenge," as Emila puts it (IV. iii. 97–98). "I would swat her off the earth's face as I would swat a moth in a cupboard" (p. 222), states Marion. The mobs too exhibit violence, hatred, and destruction. This is most unusual since Tey's novels usually lack venom or emotion.

Secondly, there is bitterness against individuals who help the undeserving and leave them to survive on their own.

the *Watchman* [liberal Newspaper] had a passion for euphemism: unrest, . . . under-privileged, backward, unfortunate; where the rest of the world talked about violence, the poor, mentally deficient, and prostitutes; and one of the things that the *Ack-Emma* and the *Watchman* had in common . . . was the belief that all prostitutes were hearts-of-gold who had taken the wrong turning. (p. 153)

Liberals apparently are childish, simple-minded, and unable to
face the true ugly facts of life. They are quite inclined to coddle
criminals who should be punished since they are morally
irreclaimable.

Your true criminal . . . has two unvarying characteristics, and it is these
two characteristics which make him a criminal. Monstrous vanity and
colossal selfishness. And they are both as integral, as the texture of the
skin. You might as well talk of "reforming" the color of one's eyes. (p.
188)

And later

Even the Bishop of Larborough would find some difficulty in thinking
up a case for her. His usual "environment" hobby-horse is no good this
time. Betty Kane had everything that he recommends for the cure of
the criminal: love, freedom to develop her talents, education, security.
It's quite a poser for his lordship when you come to consider it, because
he doesn't believe in heredity. He thinks that criminals are made, and
therefore can be unmade. "Bad Blood" is just an old superstition, in the
Bishop's estimation. (pp. 222–223)

Again, in her previous novels, the criminals acted from basically
sensible motives, were "first offenders," or were hopelessly mad.
In fact, it is difficult to dislike Tey's murderers. It is as if
something in her personal life persuaded her to react strongly
and emotionally to the facts of the Canning story.

CHAPTER 9

To Love and Be Wise

*T*O *Love and Be Wise*[1] was published in 1951, approximately one year before the death of Josephine Tey. Once again Inspector Grant is featured, along with Marta Hallard, the actress and two writers mentioned in *The Daughter of Time*, Silas Weekley and Lavinia Fitch. As in *Brat Farrar*, Tey uses a situation that seems initially not only unlikely, but impossible: the handsome and attractive Leslie Searle with whom Walter Whitmore plans to write a book is in fact a woman. Furthermore, no one even notices or suspects it. This glancing look at sexual deviance is handled discreetly and tactfully in the best traditions of the Golden Age. Yet Tey's careful and detailed sketching of even minor characters and her probing insights into motivation place *To Love and Be Wise* in the mainstream of present-day literature.

I *The Plot*

At a literary party for Lavinia Fitch, Grant meets Leslie Searle, a handsome, "disconcerting" photographer. Lavinia invites Searle to Salcott St. Mary for the weekend to meet her nephew. Walter is "the British Public's bright boy," a radio commentator who fancies himself a genius. Marta comments:

My dear, I hate the way he *yearns*. It was bad enough when he was yearning over the thyme on an Aegean hillside with the bullets zipping past his ears—he never failed to let us hear the bullets: I always suspected that he did it by cracking a whip—. (p. 12)

Previously engaged to Marguerite Merriam, an actress who committed suicide, Walter is now engaged to "Dear, nice Liz" Garrowby, Lavinia's secretary. On the drive to the country, Liz is

127

surprised to find herself speaking openly and even intimately
with Searle.

Why had she told him that, she wondered? Why had she told him that
her mother was possessive; even if she had made it clear that she was
possessive in the very nicest way? Was it possible that she was nervous?
She, who was never nervous and never chattered. (p. 19)

Salcott St. Mary is a memorable example of the closed,
innocent society referred to by W. H. Auden in "The Guilty
Vicarage."[2] Isolated from the main stream of traffic, the town has
been taken over by artists.

Every third cottage in the place has an alien in it. All degrees of wealth,
from Toby Tullis—the playwright, you know—who has a lovely
Jacobean house in the middle of the village street, to Serge Ratoff the
dancer who lives in a converted stable. . . . All degrees of talent from
Silas Weekley, who writes those dark novels of Country life, all
steaming manure and slashing rain, to Miss Easton-Dixon who writes a
fairy-tale book once a year for the Christmas trade. (p. 22)

When they arrive, Liz is surprisingly relieved that the drive is
over. Emma Garrowby, Liz's mother, dislikes Searle at sight,
assuming him to be a threat to the carefully arranged engagement between Walter and her daughter.
    Walter, however, neither introspective nor shrewd, is
delighted and enthralled by Searle. He revels in the photographer's interest, though occasionally he is disconcerted by a
chance phrase or word. Nonetheless, he delights in introducing
Searle to the local celebrities. It is here that Tey draws
especially delightful and damning sketches of playwrights,
writers, actors, and dancers. Toby Tullis, for example, a
successful playwright, is crass and insensitive. He has what Tey
chooses to call "a spiritual astigmatism" (p. 43). "Marta Hallard
had once said: 'Everything that Toby does is just a little off-key,'
and that described it very well" (p. 44).
    In describing Silas Weekley, Tey contemptuously dismisses the
"earthier" writers as well as their public.

Weekley resented beauty, and it was not entirely to be held against him
that he made a very large income out of that resentment. His
resentment was quite genuine. The world he approved was, as Liz had

said, "all steaming manure and slashing rain." . . . . His lecture tours in America were wild successes, not so much because his earnest readers in Peoria and Paducah loved steaming manure but because Silas Weekley looked the part so perfectly. He was cadaverous, and dark, and tall, and his voice was slow and sibilant and hopeless, and all the good ladies of Peoria and Paducah longed to take him home and feed him up and give him a brighter outlook on life. In which they were a great deal more generous than his English colleagues: who considered him an unmitigated bore and a bit of an ass. (p. 45)

To complete her coterie of authors, Tey includes Miss Easton-Dixon and Lavinia Fitch. Miss Easton-Dixon writes a fairy tale once a year for the Christmas trade and spends the remainder of her time avidly reading film magazines and attending the cinema. Was this a mocking and critical self-portrait? Tey's contempt for her own novels and enjoyment of films are established facts. Lavinia Fitch writes what is currently termed "Gothic novels;" that is, the heroine, always innocent and beautiful, endures a series of harrowing and predictable experiences, usually in a dark and gloomy mansion, and emerges, innocence intact, to marry the handsome stranger. Tey's opinion of Gothic novels is obvious, for even Lavinia refers to her heroine as "idiotic."

Customarily, the male members of the artistic ménage meet at the Swan, a local pub. (Interestingly, Tey's women seldom drink and generally confine themselves to sherry when they do.) Searle enjoys playing with the inflated egos of Tullis and Weekley, ignoring the former and flattering the latter. Tullis is amazed: "no one had been rude to Toby Tullis for at least a decade" (p. 43) Weekley is simply a bewildered victim of Searle's charm. There is, as Tey describes it, an almost "feminine dexterity" (p. 46) about the photographer's behavior as well as a ruthless cruelty. These traits, in fact, are the central motivating forces behind Searle's behavior.

Serge Ratoff, broken-down dancer and sycophant to Tullis, becomes enraged at this shabby treatment of his hero and attacks Searle, calling him a "Middle West Lucifer" (p. 49). He is quickly and easily rebuffed and removed from the pub. Tey handles Ratoff and the homosexual overtones of the theater community with a light touch, neither ignoring the fact nor drawing undue attention to it. She does stress, however, the oddness of Liz's attraction to Searle. He attracts and fascinates her. He is a Lucifer, a beautiful demon, dangerous, charming, and graceful. There is, as Tey continually protests, a "feeling of — wrongness" (p. 72). A psychoanalytically oriented critic might insist that Tey protests too much; that she saw the lesbian attraction as at once very appealing and terrifying. No known facts from her life support it.

Walter and Searle plan to do a book together, using the Rushmere River as a connecting motif. Walter will burble about the beauties of the river while Searle photographs them. The easiest approach, they decide, is to canoe down the river. Walter, though insensitive and egocentric, is more and more vaguely and unaccountably discomfited by Searle's presence. His program is not its usual success.

Today his guest was a child who kept a tame fox, and Walter was dismayed to find himself disliking the brat. Walter loved his guests. He felt warm and protective and all-brothers-together about them . . . He loved them to the point of tears. And now it upset him to feel detached and critical about Harold Dibbs and his silly fox. (p. 59)

When he returns to Trimmings, the home he shares with his Aunt Lavinia and Liz and Emma Garrowby, he discovers that Liz and Searle had missed his broadcast. They had been sightseeing. Walter is further disturbed to discover that Searle has bought Liz a large, expensive, and elaborate box of chocolates. He himself had brought her a small box which had gone unnoticed.

Even Lavinia Fitch, normally placid and unexcitable, feels troubled by Searle's presence. Walter's own resentment grows daily, increased by Liz's determination to be extra kind. "But for all the subterranean tremors that agitated Trimmings—Lavinia's misgiving, Walter's resentment, Liz's feeling of guilt, Emma's hatred—life on the surface was smooth" (p. 80).

Walter and Searle set out on their trip late Friday after dinner. Each night, they report to Trimmings by phone since Walter insists that they are "to be as strangers in a strange land, passing down the river and through Salcott St. Mary as though they had never seen it before" (p. 82). Initially, they seem excited by their adventure. On Wednesday they camp out near Salcott and stop that evening at the Swan. The other customers notice "something personal and urgent in their intercourse [that] kept the others, almost unconsciously, from joining them" (p. 83). Walter leaves suddenly and angrily. Searle, however, remains until closing, explaining that Walter was very annoyed with him.

Two days later Grant arrives at Trimmings to investigate the disappearance of Leslie Searle. The photographer had left the pub and never been seen again. He is presumed drowned, but the body cannot be located. This is an ironic reversal of Tey's earliest novels in which there was a body, but identification was missing. Here there is an identifiable personality, but his body is missing.

Grant carefully considers the possibilities: suicide, accident, murder, or perhaps "the fellow just ducked" (p. 95). Foreshadowing the climax of the novel, Grant insists: "There's a strong aroma of the sawn lady about this. Or don't you smell it?" (p. 88). Williams, his well-trained assistant, admits it is "a very queer set up" (p. 88).

At Trimmings, Grant interviews everyone. Walter, in sharp contrast to his usual effusive behavior, is subdued and confused. Lavinia and Liz feel very much at loose ends, while Emma is simply relieved. Grant, in traditional detective fashion, searches Searle's room and luggage. He discovers in a photographic material box an empty space, ten inches long by three and a half by four. Whatever had neatly filled the hole when Searle arrived was missing. Secondly, Grant finds a glove of Liz's which he assumes to be an old-fashioned love object. This is, of course, another of the detective's erroneous conclusions.

No evidence of Searle is discovered at bus or railway stations. Williams, always the advocate of the obvious solutions, insists Searle is in the river and Walter put him there. Grant clings like a determined terrier to his belief that the disappearance was voluntary, though there are no clues to support his theory.

Grant sends out an S.O.S. on the radio to see if a passing motorist might have picked up the missing man. He also inquires into Searle's background from the San Francisco police. Always methodical, the Inspector then begins to establish everyone's alibi. Liz had gone to her room, presumably to sort out her conflicting feelings, and Lavinia too had gone to bed early. Emma had attended a meeting and strolled home alone, not far from the camp. The housemaid can supply no additional information except "Mr. Searle was the only one she had ever met who considered a girl's feet . . . . He would say 'You can do this or that and that will save you coming up again, won't it'" (p.

127). This is meant of course to be a direct clue to Searle's real sex since no Englishman "ever cared two hoots whether you had to come up again or not" (p. 127).

Even those in the village whom Searle had met and antagonized had had poor alibis. Serge was dancing alone by the river, choreographing a new ballet. Tullis was discussing a play with his latest protégé (who clearly would corroborate anything the playwright said). Silas Weekley maintains that he was writing a new novel, a statement no one can prove or disprove. Since no one had an ironclad alibi, the astute reader well versed in the genre can be sure that none of the suspects is guilty.

That evening Grant contacts Searle's cousin in London and makes an appointment for the following day. To Marta, he ticks off the logical explanations for Searle's disappearance.

The possibilities are: one, that he fell into the river accidentally and was drowned; two, that he was murdered and thrown in the river; three, that he walked away for reasons of his own; four, that he wandered away because he forgot who he was and where he was going; and five, that he was kidnapped. (p. 162)

He asks Marta her opinion, knowing

It was true that actors had a perception, an understanding of human motive, that normal people lacked. It had nothing to do with intelligence, and very little to do with education. In general knowledge Marta was as deficient as a not very bright child of eleven; her attention automatically slid off anything that was alien to her own immediate interests and the result was an almost infantile ignorance. (p. 167)

Tey apparently, had very ambivalent feelings toward actors, seeing them as generally competent on stage, but selfish and unreliable off. Personally, she shied away from the leading actors and actresses of her plays, preferring to mingle, if necessary, with the "bit" players.

Marta insists that Emma Garrowby is the likeliest candidate for murderer. Emma wanted her daughter to marry the wealthy and established Walter. She was single-minded enough to commit murder if her plans were threatened. Grant is delighted to have Emma as chief suspect since it simplifies matters immensely. "It required immense ingenuity to find a reason why Leslie Searle should have chosen to disappear. It needed no ingenuity at all to suggest why Emma Garrowby should have killed him" (p. 173).

The following morning, just as he is about to leave for the London interview with Searle's cousin, Marta calls and insists he come over immediately. Had he proceeded to London, of course, the problem would have been quickly solved and the novel ended without the suspense of redragging the river. Tommy Thrupp, the housekeeper's son, fished up Searle's shoe from the river. Williams is sent on to London, and Grant organizes a new search party. He himself supervises the dragging of the river, but nothing is found. The San Francisco police report is of little help, and events have ground to the traditional halt. In all of Tey's novels, the detective reaches a point in which the leads fail and the clues are misleading or confusing. This is the traditional "dark before the dawn."

Before returning empty-handed to London, Grant again interviews Walter, learning only that Searle received no mail and that Emma knew the exact location of their camp the night of the disappearance. Disconcerted and frustrated, Grant returns home.

Suddenly, six days later, the pieces fall abruptly into place. Grant then delights in scurrying about asking enigmatic questions. Finally, he calls on Lee Searle, Leslie's so-called cousin. After a brief parrying, Grant elicits a confession. Having discovered early in her career as a photographer that life was less complicated if she dressed like a man, she continued to do so except for a few months she spent in England as a woman, practicing her painting skills.

The empty space in the box had held her women's shoes, and the glove, not a love object, was to be part of her disguise when escaping. A close cousin of Marguerite Merriam, whose suicide was supposedly motivated by Walter, she vowed revenge.

She had planned to murder Walter and then disappear forever into the role of Lee Searle. However, when she met Liz and learned from Marta the true personality of Marguerite, she was dissuaded.

But the Marguerite that Marta and those other people knew was someone I didn't know at all . . . Marta said: "The trouble was that she didn't allow anyone else to [live]. The suction she created," Marta said, "was so great that her neighbors were left in a vacuum. They either

expired for suffocation or they were dashed to death against the
nearest large object." (p. 244)

She ultimately realized her plan was foolish. It was impossible
to be enamored of a person like Marguerite and still have
judgment—impossible to love and be wise.

The critics were scarcely unanimous in their responses to this
novel. The *New York Times* reviewer insisted "Miss Tey can do
much better."[3] The *New York Herald Tribune* agreed that it is "a
rather slim story."[4] But the strongest objection came from Earle
F. Walbridge who insisted that the novel "fetches up with a
solution so staggeringly unlikely that credulity and mystery
collapse like a house of cards."[5]

II *Plotting Devices*

Yet the plot, when compared with Tey's earlier novels, is much
more polished and systematic, using the type of foreshadowing
and ironic symbolism found, for example, in *Miss Pym Disposes.*

Initially the plot resembles *Brat Farrar* in which a young
American stranger appears in an established British family and
community. The society which he enters is closed, innocent in
terms of the knowledge of death, and isolated. The action is
focussed entirely in this small area until the climax of the novel
and Grant's incredible discovery in London.

III *Characterization*

Again, the "stranger" is both villain and victim, though Searle
is admittedly only an apparent victim. This outsider appears to
be something he is not, and this masquerade inevitably results in
an increased self-knowledge and awareness for the immediate
family. Brat Farrar appeared to be Patrick, the missing brother,
and his search for the truth about his look-alike reveals the
extent of Simon's perfidy. Here Searle appears to be a man and
by his disappearance subdues the often irritating Walter and
clarifies Liz's feelings toward him.

Other characters seem familar from the earlier novel. Aunt
Bee returns in the incarnation of Lavinia Fitch, a slightly
muddle-headed, but successful novelist. Eleanor, attracted to
the fatal Brat Farrar, is like Liz who finds Searle both exciting

and terrifying (the latter no doubt is to reassure the reader of her "normality" and innocence which are prerequisites for Tey's heroine). From Tey's earliest novels, *The Man in the Queue* and *A Shilling for Candles*, reappears the slightly irritating, often fatuous young man whose egocentricity gets him into difficulties. As in the previous novels, the young man is suspected of murder, though in this case Grant does not exert himself to build a case. Finally, the author includes the familar Marta Hallard, previously "remote" but now sometimes "sensitive," and Sergeant Williams, Grant's faithful assistant and dogsbody.

Furthermore, the characters fit neatly into Tey's favorite subroles. The women are all motherly and kindly. Lavinia fears for Liz's emotions as much as Emma worries about her physical comfort in the future. Liz treats Walter like a small boy who needs pampering. Walter is the naive, if irritating, young man in need of perennial mothering.

> But it did not matter very much, Grant thought, that Walter did not know very much about Liz. Liz, he was quite sure, knew all that was to be known about Walter, and that was a very good basis for a happy married life. (p. 235)

Grant himself is fed and comforted by Marta in this novel as he is by cousin Laura in *The Singing Sands.*

> You feel that way only because you are tired and hungry; and probably suffering from dyspepsia, anyhow, after having to eat at the White Hart for two days. I'm going to leave you with the sherry decanter and go down and get the wine . . . She went away and Grant blessed her that she had not plagued him with the questions that must have crowded her mind. She was a woman who not only appreciated good food and good drink but was possessed of that innate good sense that is half-way to kindness. (pp. 154-155)

Of Tey's ability for characterization, there is never any doubt. "Miss Tey's style and her knack for creating bizarre characters are among the best in the field."[6] Initially Tey uses the same cleverly understated technique for character development seen in *The Daughter of Time.* Individuals are "talked about" by various other characters whose judgments we trust or learn to trust. Grant and Marta, for example, thoroughly analyze Walter long before he appears in the novel.

When we were *all* being shot at, Walter took care that he was safe in a nice fuggy office fifty feet underground. Then when it was once more unique to be in danger, up comes Walter from his little safe office and sits himself on a thymey hillside with a microphone and a whip to make bullet noises with. (p. 13)

Later, Walter is described by Williams as a "pushee" not a "pusher" (p. 91).

Secondly, the author traditionally presents the characters in speech and action. They enter and exit as in a stage production, revealing pertinent facts about themselves as they react to situations. Using the omniscient narrator point of view, Tey pries and pokes at their psyches, exposing heretofore unknown or unexpected tendences and feelings. Walter, for example, who had been far too self-centered to even consider jealousy, finds himself surprisingly antagonistic toward Searle. We learn that Grant, under the brusque Scots exterior, has a poetic soul.

" 'Swift beauty come to pass
Has drowned the blades that strove,' "
Grant said.
"What is that?"
"What an army friend of mine wrote about floods." (p. 185)

Furthermore, we learn that, like Lord Peter Wimsey, he has an awareness of good food and is proud of it. Finally, we are reminded that Grant, like Campion, Wimsey, and Inspector Alleyn, is a "gentlemen cop," one with an independent income, ("a luxury grumble, since he could have retired years ago when his aunt left him her money") (p. 178).

Significantly, the minor characters, those "bizarre" individuals who live in Salcott St. Mary, add color and depth to the action. Concentrating on writers and actors, the two types she should know best, Tey is generally uncomplimentary. Toby Tullis and Serge Ratoff, whose homosexual tendencies are delicately left unstated, emerge as self-centered and a trifle absurd. Walter is in many respects a more carefully developed variation of Tullis who is convinced both of his own fame and beauty.

"My name is Tullis. I write plays." The modesty of this phrase always enchanted him. It was as if the owner of a transcontinental railroad were to say: "I run trains." (p. 4)

While Lavinia writes Gothic novels about innocent, attractive heroines beset by trials and terrors (ironically the situation in which Liz finds herself), Silas Weekley prefers the more realisitc dirt-and-manure style. Since Tey was quite self-critical of her own novelistic efforts, her reactions to these writers is not surprising. The writers are all "a little crazy," revealing in their works their true personalities.

One of the most famous alienists in the country had once said to him that to write a book was to give oneself away. (Someone else had said the same thing more wittily and more succinctly, but he could not think at the moment who it was.) There was unconscious betrayal in every line, said the alienist. What, wondered Grant, would the alienist's verdict be after reading one of Silas Weekley's malignant effusions? (p. 149)

More interesting is the author's attempt to deal with Searle, a transvestite. Tey insists throughout that something is wrong, dangerous and untrustworthy, perhaps even evil about Searle. "Lucifer. A fallen glory. A beauty turned evil" (p. 61). Probably because of Tey's own personal animosities and fears, Searle lacks the reality of most of her characters. Like St. Joan, Searle found dressing in men's clothing both convenient and preferable. Yet the resolution to give up photography and become a woman painter is not really explained. Furthermore, the extreme attachment to Marguerite Merriam scarcely appears normal. As Walter points out, speaking of Ratoff and Tullis, "perhaps the old saying is true and it is not possible to love and be wise. When you are as devoted to anyone as Serge is to Toby Tullis, I expect you cease to be sane about the matter" (p. 51). Since the relationship between the dancer and playwright was probably homosexual, Tey is suggesting that Searle's relationship to Merriam was possibly lesbian. Searle was "so devoted that you couldn't think quite straight about her" (p. 240). Yet Searle is scarcely punished for any of her actions, nor does she feel serious remorse. Like Beau Nash in *Miss Pym Disposes* and Brat in *Brat Farrar*, the "criminal" is neatly excused, although the author does make her usual remarks concerning the freedom and pampering of criminals.

There are quite a few people I would willingly have killed in my time.

Indeed, with prison no more penitential than a not very good public
school, and the death sentence on the point of being abolished, I think
I'll make a little list, 'a la Gilbert'. Then when I grow a little aged I shall
make a total sweep—ten or so for the price of one—and retire
comfortably to be well-cared-for the rest of my life. (p. 250)

IV   *Stylistic Devices*

Tey's use of stylistic devices such as foreshadowing and ironic
symbolism add to the dimensions of her characters as well as
increasing the momentum of the action. In chapter one, for
example, the foreshadowing is extensive and intricate. The
reader is supplied with Searle's "strangeness" and motive, and
Walter's superficiality; the preparation is made for the long
search for Searle's body.

"I don't think safe is the adjective I would apply to Searle, somehow,"
he said reflectively; and from that moment forgot all about Leslie
Searle until the day when he was sent down to Salcott St. Mary to
search for the young man's body. (pp. 15–16)

V   *Symbolism*

Later, Leslie Searle is called "disconcerning," "unreal," and
most interestingly, "I'm sure that he was something very wicked
in Ancient Greece" (p. 31). Finally, the theme of disguise is
picked up in a leitmotif regarding a thief who posed as an Arab
potentate. Even the most imperceptive reader would recognize
that there was something quite "wrong" about Leslie Searle.

The ironic symbolism at which Tey excels points to the
denouement and accentuates the effects of events on the
characters' personalities. For example, the single glove suggests
at once, even to Grant, a love object belonging to one's adored
lady. And traditionally it would be regarded as such. Yet, with a
deft reversal, it becomes a symbol both of femininity and the
lack of a beloved. That lack, caused as Searle believed by
Walter, inspired and motivated her. The empty space in Searle's
box naturally suggests an equally empty place in her life which is
filled ironically by women's shoes and lipstick.

Finally, Tey again uses geographical symbols. The village, for example, isolated and odd, reflects the lives of its inhabitants, few of whom could successfully relate to other human beings. Grant, Marta, Liz, Walter, Searle, Tullis, Weekley all suffer from an isolation of spirit. They cannot intimately interrelate through their own barriers.

As the house burning in *The Franchise Affair* symbolized a cleansing of spirit, so the river in *To Love and Be Wise* suggests a rebirth for the two who travelled on it, Walter and Searle. The river is "swift Beauty," a "final Beauty" that is death. Its mud swallows up whatever comes its way. Leslie Searle, the man, is swallowed up metaphorically and so is Walter. Neither will be the same again. "Well, I've made him over for her. I'll be surprised if he isn't a new man from now on" (p. 252).

VI *Title Symbolism*

The title of this novel is taken from Shakespeare's *Troilus and Cressida* (III, ii, 163). Cressida says to her lover Troilus in a seduction scene, "for to be wise and love exceeds man's might; that dwells with gods above." Troilus then comments that this is especially true for women. Tey disagrees and illustrates her point with Toby Tullis and Serge Ratoff. Surprisingly, the problem never arises in a man / woman relationship in her novels.

VII *Themes*

As in many of her previous novels, Tey again centers on the theme "in place of another." Like Brat Farrar, Leslie Searle impersonates a non-living individual. But we see very little of the agony and suffering most of Tey's characters usually endure. Walter's discomfort at being suspected of murder and Liz's confused feelings about Searle surely do not rank with the destruction of Innes's life in *Miss Pym Disposes* or the torment of Marion and her mother in *The Franchise Affair*.

Yet, again, Tey does reflect a distrust and disbelief in appearances. No one is quite as reliable as he seems. Liz, for example, could indeed by flattered away from Walter, and her mother, a kindly quiet woman, could hold murder in her heart. Most obviously, Searle is not what he appears to be, though aside from the sexual issue, the facts overlap and blur. He was indeed a photographer who looked like "a Lucifer," a strikingly handsome individual. She was also a painter and an interesting attractive woman, talented and articulate in both incarnations. The reader is inclined to have feelings as divided as those of the author. Tye insists that tranvestism is abnormal, yet Searle is so likable that both Liz and Grant are attracted to him / her. It seems as though Tey was attempting to come to terms with her lack of faith in appearances, her distrust of people. It remains for her final three novels to confirm or deny her success.

CHAPTER 10

The Daughter of Time

THE Daughter of Time (1951) is Tey's second attempt at historical detection. Unlike John Dickson Carr who transports his detectives to the period of the crime, Tey reverses the process and brings the crime to the detective. She is unique in the use of this format.

Historical mysteries have long fascinated writers. For example, John Dickson Carr studied the mystery of Judge Godfrey in *The Murder of Sir Edmund Godfrey* (1936) and Lillian de la Torre fictionalized the Canning case in *Elizabeth is Missing* (1945). Geoffrey Bocca studied but did not solve the mystery of the strange death of Harry Oakes in the Bahamas in *The Life and Death of Sir Harry Oakes* (1959). A source book for writers of historical fiction was compiled by Kenneth B. Platnick. He summarizes sixteen unsolved cases of murder, intrigue, and disappearances in *Great Mysteries of History* (1971). In *The Franchise Affair*, Tey rewrote the Canning mystery in modern terms and solved the case. The relationship between detection and historical scholarship is closer than many historians might care to admit. The same processes of tireless investigation, painstaking sifting of information, and careful analysis of source reliability apply to both areas. Indeed, as Tey illustrates, the historian as well as the detective must consider the usefulness and authenticity of hearsay information as well as discriminating between the prejudices and opinions of sources. R. W. Weeks in *The Historian as Detective* (1968) discusses the use of evidence in scholarship as well as detection and includes a series of essays interesting to both historian and the reader of detective fiction.

I   *The Critics*

The Daughter of Time was undoubtedly Tey's most famous

141

work. It was published in 1951 shortly before her death in 1952. At the time of its publication, the novel was greeted with delight by the critics. In London, the *Times Literary Supplement* insisted "Miss Tey . . . accomplishes her task, whether of whitewashing or of creative reconstruction, with agreeable zest and the genuine entertainer's wish to please."[1] In the United States, the most prominent critics in the detective mystery fiction genre found *The Daughter of Time* unique and compelling. Tey, according to Anthony Boucher, "recreates the intense dramatic excitement of the scholarly research necessary" to unveil historical truth:

The result is a real *bouleversement* of schoolbook and encyclopedia "history," treated with compelling logic, precise scholarship and a cumulative intensity which makes the fictional, and even the factual, crimes of 1952 seem drab affairs indeed.[2]

James Sandoe adds:

This is the sort of especially satisfying book we have been led to expect from Miss Tey . . . and it gains its delight principally in the warmth and discernment of her observation of people and things. It is a rather special gift and if a more enchanting book comes my way this year I shall be surprised.[3]

Of the novels reviewed in the same articles as *The Daughter of Time* only Agatha Christie's *Mrs. McGinty's Dead* retains the same fame and popularity as Tey's novel. In the late 1950s, Howard Haycraft, historian and critic of the classical detective story, added *The Daughter of Time* to a list of the Hundred Best Crime stories. Only Julian Symons in *Bloody Murder* (1972) finds the work dull, an "amateur rehashing of a well-known argument," and adds, "Grant's almost total ignorance of history is the most remarkable thing about the book. The pleasure taken by critics in the very slow unfolding of a thesis already well known suggests a similar ignorance on their part."[4] It is doubtful that readers would agree with Mr. Symons.

II   *The Plot*

In *The Daughter of Time,* Tey's detective is once again Inspector Grant who reviews the historical accounts of the murder of the princes by Richard III. He then re-solves the crime from his sick bed. The title of the novel is taken from an old proverb, "Truth is the Daughter of Time," and Grant, centuries after the crime, ferrets out what he and many historians believe to be the truth. This is the first novel by Tey in which detailed detection is the cornerstone of plot and action.

Initially and throughout the novel Grant is in the hospital, flat on his back from injury incurred while capturing an escaping criminal. Having quickly gone through the amusements of an invalid, he is bored and ill-tempered. Marta Hallard, the actress seen briefly in *A Shilling for Candles* (1936) and *To Love and Be Wise* (1950), arrives with more books for him, including those by Lavinia Fitch and Silas Weekley, familar from the latter work. Marta in *The Daughter of Time* is more practical, articulate, and less self-centered than previously. She suggests that Grant set his mind to resolving "an unsolved problem."[5]

He instantly rejects Mary Queen of Scots. "I could be interested in a bad woman but never in a silly one" (p. 10). He continues, "Her tragedy was that she was born a queen with the outlook of a suburban housewife" (11). This attitude previously emerged in the Daviot play *Queen of Scots*. Marta leaves with the threat, "I shall look in, in a day or two, and start you on a sock. There is nothing so soothing, I understand, as knitting. Isn't that so, nurse?" (p. 14).

But instead of knitting, Marta returns with pictures of faces, Lucretia Borgia, Louis XVII, and the Earl of Leicester, among others. Grant has always been interested in faces, maintaining that a criminal could be identified by facial characteristics. This oversimplification is familar in Tey. In *The Franchise Affair*, for example, Kane is immediately picked out as a trollop by the color of her eyes and her innocent look. Grant is instantly intrigued by the picture of Richard III. A passing surgeon suggests that the picture is not one of villainy but of illness.

It's the look one sees on the face of a crippled child. If he was born a hunchback that probably accounts for it and not polio. I notice the artist has left out the hump. (p. 22)

The mystery, Grant recalls, was the disappearance of Richard's nephews and heirs to the throne. The boys were supposedly murdered by their uncle or one of his minions. Fascinated, he borrows two school history books from a nurse and begins reading.

The following day Sergeant Williams appears and Grant asks him to look at the picture of Richard III.

> "Well, where would you place him? In the dock or on the bench?" Williams considered for a moment, and then said with confidence: "Oh, on the bench."
>
> . . ."He's the spit of old Halsbury, come to think of it and if Halsbury had a fault at all it was that he was too soft with the bastards in the dock. He used to lean over backwards to give them the benefit in his summing-up." (p. 33)

This, of course, is the fault with which Tey credits Richard. Here, as in her other novels, Tey relies on the opinions of "solid citizens" for character judgments. In *The Franchise Affair*, for example, Kane was condemned by Stanley, the garage mechanic, long before the truth was known. Likewise the Sharpes were exonerated by Nevil, their lawyer's cousin and an outspoken liberal.

Comforted and reassured by Williams's opinions, Grant asks his friend to get more history books. In the books he has been reading the accounts of Richard's actions are based on Sir Thomas More's report. More, it appears, asserts that Tyrrell, friend and cohort of Richard, did the actual murders by suffocating the princes. Matron, however, adds to the favorable character description. Grant asks her:

> "So you don't think he was an out-and-out villain?"
> "No; oh, no. Villains don't suffer, and that face is full of the most dreadful pain." (p. 37)

Later Williams returns with a history of England and a slick biography of Richard's mother. Grant discovers only a few dry facts in the traditional history, among them that Richard was devoted to his brother, Edward IV. He also discovers the author quoting a contemporary writing in France. "The English never drink water except for penance" (p. 43).

In desperation at the sparsity of facts, Grant sends a note to Marta asking her to locate More's history of Richard III. Acting as a true scholar (and detective), the Inspector pursues the truth next in *The Rose of Raby*, an historical biography of Richard's mother.

It was Grant's belief that if you could not find out about a man, the next best way to arrive at an estimate of him was to find out about his mother. (p. 45)

Apparently the woman had been fond of her husband since they frequently travelled together, an uncommon occurrence in the period. Furthermore, the family was very close and devoted. Grant reads on, scanning for information on Richard and his brother. He discovers a few, very salient facts: Richard was devoted to his brother, Edward, who married a court lady much against the wishes and advice of his family. By irritating his cousin Warwick, Edward was dethroned. Richard went with him into exile, and it was Richard and his sister Margaret who organized their brother's return to England.

Next Grant reads Sir Thomas More's book and is surprised at its contents.

An aroma of back-stair gossip and servants' spying came off the page. So that one's sympathy tilted before one was aware of it from the smug commentator to the tortured creature sleepless on his bed. The murderer seemed of greater stature than the man who was writing of him. (p. 55)

More carefully catalogues Richard's tempers, paranoia, fury, and "calculated iniquity." Yet, Richard was well-liked, a competent administrator and brilliant campaigner. Grant finds the two personalities hard to integrate.

Suddenly Grant remembers a fact that makes More a prejudiced and perhaps unreliable witness. Living during the reign of Henry VIII, More had been eight years old when Richard died. His evidence then was hearsay and old hearsay at that. Anxiously, Grant pursued his study.

I want to know what made him tick. That is a more profound mystery than anything I have come up against of late. What changed him almost overnight? Up to the moment of his brother's death he seems to have been entirely admirable. (pp. 67-68)

Marta, to Grant's utmost delight, sends him an American research assistant who functions as his Watson throughout the investigation. Brent Carradine supplies Grant with contemporary history books in which is discovered a deep ambivalence toward Richard. One historian, for example, says, "He was an admirable administrator and general, with an excellent reputation, staid and good-living" (p. 76). And yet later adds that Richard was "perfectly unscrupulous and ready to wade through any depth of bloodshed to the crown" (p. 76). Perhaps most important to Grant's case is the fact that there was no mention of the murders in any writings during Richard's reign or when Henry got control of the kingdom. "What it means is that there was *no contemporary accusation at all*" (p. 81). This in spite of the fact that public knowledge of the crime would have definitely aided Henry's cause. Grant finally asks the armchair detective's most important question: "Who benefits?" (p. 84) Richard had nothing to gain from the murder since there were so many other heirs, many of whom survived him. Carradine calls More "The mean, burbling, insinuating old bastard" (p. 97).

Discovering that Edward IV's children by Elizabeth Woodville were probably illegitimate because of an earlier secret marriage by the king, the two detectives unearth reports of the plot against Richard's life and the subsequent beheading of Hastings. Yet none of Richard's actions appeared vindictive. In the tradition of the armchair detective, Grant studies first the character witnesses who speak for and against the accused. Then he studies the clues, that is, the reports and letters written by contemporaries. Finally, the detectives review the action of the accused and those about him.

Grant is quite satisfied that

From the police point of view there is no case against Richard at all. And I mean that literally. It isn't that the case isn't good enough. Good enough to bring into court, I mean. There, quite literally, isn't any case against him at all. (p. 121)

Logically the next question is "Who did murder the boys?" (p. 122) Grant now runs up against the usual hitch in detective fiction, the one small fact that seems to blow up the case— rumors of the princes' deaths occurred before Richard's destruction in battle. Grant successfully proves that Morton, enemy of Richard, carried the tale, thus making it immediately suspect. Furthermore, the later Tyrrell "confession" is suspect. Tyrrell confessed to the crime twenty years after it took place and "Nothing was heard of Tyrrell's confession until Tyrrell was dead" (p. 141). Searching for a "break in the pattern," Carradine and Grant discover that the boys' mother was free to visit court under Richard's reign but was confined to a convent by Henry.

Lining up the clues, Grant is convinced of Henry's guilt. Carradine, however, discovers the theory is an old one. Grant nonetheless persuades him to write a book about Richard vindicating him and crusading against what he terms "tonypandy." It should be noted that Tey herself, under the Daviot name, continued a personal crusade against "tonypandy" which began with her biography of Claverhouse and ended with *The Privateer*, which supposedly cleared the name of Henry Morgan once and for all.

Whether or not the view of history Tey presents is accurate is basically insignificant in a study of her style and technique. The historical viewpoint known as "Ricardian" has had, as the author points out, supporters for several centuries. Among them recently is Thomas Costain in *The Last of the Plantagenets*.

III   *The Rules*

What is significant and unique in *The Daughter of Time* is the complete "breaking of the rules," so to speak. For example, no one involved in the murder or slander is living or presented in action. In fact, there is no action at all in the novel. And yet it is suspenseful, compelling, and absorbing. Tey accomplishes what most biographers and historians hope for but seldom achieve. She involves the reader in a living and exciting history.

How is this done? First, Tey uses the popular approach developed by Edgar Allan Poe and Conan Doyle and perfected by Agatha Christie, that of the "armchair detective." To illustrate the popularity of this viewpoint, one need only mention that the only significant periodical devoted to a comprehensive, critical study of detective fiction is entitled *The Armchair Detective*.

The structure of this novel can be roughly outlined as follows. First, the detective is doubtful as to the guilt of the accused. In Christie's *Mrs. McGinty's Dead*, published at approximately the same time as *The Daughter of Time*, the doubt is initially voiced to Poirot by Inspector Spence who feels that James Bentley is "just not the type." Inspector Grant begins by being fascinated by a picture of Richard III. As proud of his ability to judge

criminals by their faces as Poirot is of his "little gray cells," Grant
becomes convinced that the King was not the monster he was
supposed to be. Next the detective begins sifting the facts. First,
he studies character reports. The children's history, with few
facts, insists Richard was a monster. A somewhat more sophisticated school history suggests that he was a good administrator,
devoted to his brother, but nonetheless greedy, ill, and evil. Yet
when Grant shows the portrait of the accused to friends, he gets
a different response.

Marta thinks he is a little like Lorenzo the Magnificent. Her friend
James thinks it is the face of a saint. My surgeon thinks it is the face of a
cripple. Sergeant Williams thinks he looks like a great judge. But I
think, perhaps, Matron comes nearest the heart of the matter. . . . She
says it is a face full of the most dreadful suffering. (p. 165)

As Grant with the help of Carradine searches on, he discovers, as
Poirot does, that negative reports are hearsay evidence, and that
eyewitness reports are highly flattering to the character of the
accused. The clues are sifted carefully and can be grouped into
two neat catagories, the physical and the psychological. Under
physical clues are letters, account books, and monk's chronicles.
In *Mrs. McGinty's Dead*, the clues are an old newspaper clipping,
a photograph, and a book. Psychological clues deal primarily
with the character of the accused. Is it likely, for example, that a
man who was a brilliant general and devoted to his brother
would cold-bloodedly and with malice aforethought murder his
nephews for no reason whatsoever?
   It appears, then, that the accused is innocent. However, at this
point the peripety or reversal occurs and a clue appears that
suggests, indeed insists on, the guilt of the accused. Shortly,
however, the clue is explained away. Now, not satisfied with
mere acquittal, the detective continues his investigation to
discover the true murderer. Most readers of traditional detective
fiction will recognize this as a familar theme. The first question
the detective then asks is always "Who benefits from the
crime?" Often, the answer appears to be no one, but this
assumption is later proved false. Next, if anyone has blatantly
accused the suspect, his motives are considered carefully and he

is discredited. Finally, the detective discovers a break in the pattern that reveals the truth.

IV   *The Character of Inspector Grant*

Another factor that ensures interest in *The Daughter of Time* is the character of Grant. The novel, told from Grant's point of view, is held together by his careful, systematic thinking and his emotional involvement, traits we have observed in previous works. Placed in an unenviable invalid's position, Grant becomes both the ideal detective and scholar. He and Carradine study the facts through all available channels, discard unreliable scholarship, and settle on a plausible theory. They then gather facts to support it. Discovering that the idea is not original does not discourage the young American from writing his book in support of the theory. Most important, Grant searches out what he feels to be the truth, the goal of both scholars and detectives. The author insists that truth will out—"Truth is the daughter of time." It is interesting to note that this is the first and only Tey novel in which the emphasis is placed on armchair detection. Furthermore, it is the only Inspector Grant novel with the exception of *The Singing Sands* in which he does not assume the guilt of an innocent person.

V   *Distrust of Appearances*

In *The Daughter of Time* Tey once again illustrates her distrust of appearance. It is known that Polydore Vergil and Henry VII rewrote history rapidly on the spot to suit themselves. Needless to say, there are a number of contemporary parallels. Tey firmly expresses her distrust of the press (she never would give press interviews) as well as of political and historical accounts of events. This alteration of facts is termed "tonypandy" and Tey cites examples in America and Scotland to prove her point. A favorite theme, she reiterates it in *Claverhouse*, *The Franchise Affair*, and *The Privateer*. Even school books, she insists, are no longer "safe," often containing misleading, distorted, and unreliable "facts." Nonetheless, Tey's touching faith in ultimate truth continues throughout all her works. The innocent may suffer temporarily, but truth will undoubtedly emerge.

VI *Institutions as Symbols*

Since character alone cannot sustain a novel, Tey creates tension by suggesting conflicting institutions. First, of course, there is the hospital, its somewhat impersonal, realistic, no-nonsense qualities illustrated by the nurses. Here in one lonely room Grant is, so to speak, imprisoned, unable to leave or even move, victim of the rules and and whims of hospital regulations. Nonetheless, the reader does not see beyond Grant's isolated room to the life-and-death mechanisms of the institution. This is, as it were, off stage.

The second institution, Scotland Yard, is represented primarily by Sergeant Williams. Grant, normally associated with it, is not directly involved in any Yard activities. The police, too, have their impersonal, realistic rules and like the nurses, Williams seeks more to humor Grant than help him. Again, activity at the Yard and its machinations of law and order are only hinted at briefly.

Marta Hallard, who begins Grant on his quest, represents a third institution, the theater. Its imaginative, creative, and unrealistic qualities are the direct opposite of either antiseptic hospital or grim police station. The frivolous, unimportant, and even absurd characters of Marta's world contrast sharply with those from the other institutions. The theater too remains remote.

Thus all the action involving the theater is reported by Marta much in the stage tradition of an announcer. Although the reader is aware of other characters, such as Carradine's fiancée, they never appear.

The same is true of the library from which Carradine returns full of news. The library is as withdrawn, isolated, unrealistic, and often pointless in aims and action as the theater. Carradine alone represents that scholarly area and ironically serves as announcer for the final institution, the kingly courts of Richard III and Henry VII. Here, unlike the other areas, there is no direct spokesman, nor are any moral or impersonal rules observed. Each reported action, including the murder, Richard's friendliness, Henry's cruelty, are based upon personal motives, individual convenience, and a hard-hearted, realistic approach to survival.

By creating so many institutions, each represented by a spokesman, Tey draws attention away from the lack of characters and action in the mystery. Each institution has its own goals and rules which conflict in many areas. For example, the hospital wishes only to see Grant eat well and recover; what amuses and interests him is of little significance. To the theater, amusement and interest are all-embracing.

VII   *The Themes*

Finally, it should be noted that Tey again reiterates several of her favorite themes. First is the English-American conflict seen in previous works. Unlike her contemporaries, who rarely consider America at all, Tey sees it as a harsh, cruel, yet somehow exciting land which demands productive work of its residents. Carradine's father will be content to see his son's book. Brat Farrar grew up and became a realistic adult on the ranch in the Southwest. Tisdale is rewarded for his sufferings with a California ranch which, it is assumed, will "make a man of him."

Secondly, as in *Claverhouse* and *The Privateer,* two of her Daviot novels, Tey whitewashes a historical figure. While the evidence indicates that Richard did not kill his nephews, it is still doubtful that he was as good, honest, brilliant, and clever as Tey suggests. Claverhouse, Morgan, and Richard seem to share the same characteristics according to the author, of brilliant tactics, leadership abilities, kindness, and sensitivity. These, it appears, sum up Tey's favorite hero. The basis of these traits in fact, however, for these three individuals is not as clear-cut as the author would have the reader believe.

Finally, as previously stated, Tey indicates her perpetual distrust of the press and impersonal institutions who prefer to accept appearances rather than truth. Since, according to Tey, appearances are always misleading, their reports are not to be trusted. There is little doubt that Tey's personal conflicts and problems are reflected in her works. It should be noted that in this novel as well as in *The Singing Sands,* which was published posthumously, Inspector Grant is seriously ill throughout most of the work. Tey herself was aware of her own fatal illness as these books were being written.

CHAPTER 11

The Singing Sands

WHEN *The Daughter of Time* was published in 1951 (Tey died in February, 1952), it was assumed that was her final novel. Yet among her papers were discovered the drafts for both *The Singing Sands* and *The Privateer. The Singing Sands* (1952) was Tey's last novel. She died before completing the final editing, which explains and forgives the few weaknesses in the work. This novel, like the three before it, features Inspector Grant. He is again ill, as in *The Daughter of Time,* but this time becomes involved in a bizarre and contemporary crime rather than a historical one. There is no question that the author's sensitive descriptive powers were at their zenith in this final detective novel.

I   *The Plot*

It was six o'clock of a March morning and still dark. The long train came sidling through the scattered lights of the yard, clicking gently over the points. Into the glow of the signal cabin and out again. Under the solitary emerald among the rubies on the signal bridge. On towards the empty grey waste of platform that waited under the arcs.[1]

Grant, on the verge of a nervous breakdown with claustrophobic symptoms, is travelling on this mail train. As he is about to leave the train, he passes a compartment where the porter, a thoroughly unpleasant person nicknamed "Old Yoghourt," is attempting to wake a passenger. Grant comments, "Can't you recognise a dead man when you see one?" (p. 9).

He looked again at the young face under the rumpled dark hair, and went away down the corridor. Dead men were not his responsibility. He had had his fill of dead men in his time, and although he had never quite lost a heart contraction at its irrevocability, death had no longer power to shock him. (p. 10).

The porter assumes that the man drank himself to death, since the smell of alcohol in the compartment is overpowering.

Grant goes to the hotel for breakfast. He discovers among his magazines and newspapers yesterday's *Clarion* with an odd verse pencilled in the "Stop Press" blank.

> The beasts that talk,
> The streams that stand,
> the stones that walk,
> The singing Sands
> . . . .
> . . . .
> That guard the way
> To Paradise. (p. 13)

Since he himself did not write the verse, he is at first bewildered. It occurs to the Inspector that he had inadvertently picked up the paper in the dead man's compartment. The handwriting intrigues him too, since it is adolescent and "pure copy book form" (p. 14).

Grant temporarily forgets about the verse as Tommy, his cousin Laura's husband, meets him and they begin their drive into the country. An automobile ride for the claustrophobic Inspector is a terrible and frightening trial. In order to keep control of himself and not bother Tommy with his illness, Grant thinks about the man in compartment B-seven.

Why had he come to the North at this bleak, unfashionable season? To fish? To climb? . . . A sailor going to join his ship? Going to some naval base beyond Inverness? That was possible.

What else was there? What would bring a dark, thin young man with reckless eyebrows and a passion for alcohol to the Highlands at the beginning of March? (p. 22)

Grant survives the automobile trip. "Grant looked down at his hands, and found that they were still. The dead man, who could not save himself, had saved him" (p. 23).

The Inspector relaxes with his cousin, a favorite type in Tey's

works. Laura is motherly, kindly, sensitive, intuitive, aware of
Grant's needs before he realizes them himself. Under this benign
influence, he becomes more at ease. Nonetheless, part of his
mind remains intrigued by the train incident.

Most of Grant's time is spent with his young nephew, Pat, an
outspoken, red-headed child with "a bleak and intimidating grey
eye" (p. 27). Pat plans to be a revolutionary at maturity and thus
is acquainted with Wee Archie, the local rabble-rouser. While
fishing, Grant meets Archie who asks if Grant knows the islands.
He does not and Archie begins telling him of the wonders to be
seen.

"The sands don't sing, I suppose," Grant said, putting bounds to the
boasting. He stepped into the boat, and pushed off. (p. 27)

After a moment, Grant shouted after him, "Are there any
walking stones in Cladda?" His reply was brief: "No, they're in
Lewis."

Meanwhile, the newspaper identifies the dead man as a
Charles Martin, a Frenchman and mechanic. Grant finds this
identification hard to believe since the handwriting was strictly
of the English schoolboy variety. Knowing his duty, the Inspector
writes Scotland Yard of his discovery of verse and handwriting.

The Yard is not interested. Grant's superior, Bryce, is cold,
insensitive, and without feeling. Angry that Grant got ill, he is
doubly irritated to be bothered with such an inconsequential
matter. Never one to give up easily, as seen in the previous
novels, Grant calls his faithful dogsbody, Williams, and ascertains
more facts. No one personally identified Martin; his family
identified him from a picture taken after death. He was a
mechanic and had several letters with him, one from a French
girl promising to wait for him. He had some English money and
no passport. Finally, his shoes were made in Karachi. The coach
attendant noticed Martin joking with a companion before
departure about "robbing the Caley," probably a hotel called
the Caledonian. Finally, he had a return ticket. The P.M. showed
a large amount of whiskey in the stomach, a fair amount in the
blood, but no tissue degeneration to indicate he was an alcoholic.

Grant spends the morning fishing, and arguing with his "voice"
who demands he forget about Martin. The voice insists:

"You were B-Seven's champion the minute you saw his face and noticed

the way that Yoghourt was mauling him about. You snatched him from
Yoghourt's grip and straightened his jacket like a mother pulling a
shawl over her baby. . . . . He was young and dead, and he had been
reckless and alive. You wanted to know what he had been like when he
was reckless and alive." (p. 61)

Becoming more and more interested in Martin, his history, and
motivations, Grant begins forgetting about his own problems, the
first step in his cure.

Grant awakens the following morning suffering from rheuma-
tism in his right shoulder. Only too aware of what "your subconscious and your body could achieve between them" (p. 67),
he knew that he had a valid excuse to avoid fishing that day. "His
subconscious had wanted to go in to Scoone today and talk to the
librarian at the public library" (p. 68). His health improving
rapidly, Grant is delighted to get into town. He first interviews
Old Yoghourt, the sleeping car attendant, and learns a very few
pieces of information about the inquest and the coroner's
verdict. He speaks to the librarian too about the singing sands on
Cladda. He learns that there are indeed "talking beasts" or seals
there and some say walking stones. But the only streams that
stood were those in a bog. Intrigued, Grant resolves to visit the
islands. Since he still suffers from claustrophobia, he plans to
take a boat, though the trip will be none too pleasant this time of
year. Before leaving, Grant puts an ad in the paper asking anyone
familiar with the lines of poetry he had found, written
presumably by the dead man, to contact him.

In the small hotel at Cladda, Grant finds his room draughty
and uncomfortable.

Two of the four drawers in the chest were capable of being opened.
The third would not open because it had lost its knob, and the fourth
because it had lost the will. Above the black iron fireplace with its frill
of red crinkled paper brown with age was an engraving of a partially
clothed Venus comforting a quite unclothed Cupid. If the cold had not
already eaten into his bones, Grant thought that the picture would have
finished the process. (pp. 77-78)

Bitterly chilled, he sits by the only fire in the office of the
proprietor, Mr. Todd. Enjoying a warming whiskey, he and Mr.
Todd discuss Cladda. The meal that night was miserable and the
rooms icy, but Grant accepts it all in good humor.

The following day he meets Father Heslop, who invites him home for tea, of the same quality he had received at the hotel. Apparently, no one on Cladda did any baking; all buns, biscuits, and breads were imported from Glasgow. Having lived in Cladda for sixteen years, Father Heslop is familiar with the island and its legends. Most people, he points out, describe Cladda as just near heaven, a far from factual description. Heslop insists that they want to see it like that or are ashamed because they don't. Grant walks to the sea and revels in its beauty.

He walked on over the fine white sand to the edge of the water, and let the tumult roar over him. At close quarters it had a senseless quality that dissolved his uncomfortable sense of diminution and made him feel human and superior. . . . He felt warm and alive and master of himself; admirably intelligent and gratifyingly sentient . . . He was h a p p y .
(p. 88)

This is one of the few instances in which Tey records Grant as actually being happy, rather than merely content or satisfied.

The following morning Grant meets the Presbyterian minister, Reverend Mr. MacKay, who is on his way to see if the crews of two fishing boats, one Swedish, the other Dutch, wished to attend church on Sunday. MacKay invites Grant to the *ceilidh*, a local get-together and dance. Grant agrees to attend and spends the day pondering over the motives of B-Seven.

. . . here was B-Seven's world, according to specifications. The singing sands, the talking beasts, the walking stones, the streams that ceased to run. What had B-Seven intended to do here? Just to come, as he himself had done, and look?
A flying dash, with an overnight case. That surely portended one of two things: a meeting or an inspection. (p. 93)

Again, as in *The Man in the Queue*, Grant is totally wrong in his premise, but he will, nonetheless, arrive at the correct solution.

That evening he enjoys the local entertainment at the *ceilidh*, as well as "a wee drop" of whiskey with the men. Tey comments on the Scots' attitude toward whiskey:

Not much wonder that the Scots were silly and arch and coy about whiskey . . . Not much wonder that they behaved as if there was something very dashing, not to say daring, about having a drink of whiskey. The surprising, the knowing leer with which the ordinary Scot referred to his national drink could only come from inherited knowledge of prohibition: either the Kirk's or the Law's. (p. 96)

Suddenly Grant notices a small odd speaker and recognizes Wee Archie. For half an hour every one listens intently to him and then slowly, people quietly file out.

"Why are they leaving?"
"They're going to watch the ballet."
"The *ballet*?"
"Television. It's their great treat. Everything else they see on television is just a version of something they've seen already. . . . But ballet is something they've never seen before." (p. 98)

Everyone returns for the dance and "a wonderful time was had by all" (p. 99). Grant notices Archie slyly smuggling something to the sailors and this too pleases him. Archie is not as perfect as he would like to appear, and the Yard has been hoping to get something on him for some time. Ironically, on his visits to Cladda, Archie rooms with the Reverend Mr. MacKay, who may or may not know of his illicit dealings. Tey, never one to favor Presbyterians judging from her opinions in *Claverhouse*, leaves the matter up to the reader regarding the Reverend MacKay's actual or unwitting involvement.

After a week on the island, Grant flies back to his cousin's. He shares the flight with Wee Archie, much to the Inspector's disgust. "The little bastard, he thought. The vain, worthless little bastard" (p. 103). Again, Tey has Grant comment on the vanity of the criminal.

The vain, vicious little bastard. He had had a profession that would give him his bread and butter, a profession that would have brought him spiritual reward. But that had not satisfied his egotistical soul. He had needed the limelight. And as long as he could strut in the light, he did not care who paid for the illumination.

Grant was still considering the fundamental part that vanity played in the make-up of the criminal when a geometrical pattern opened below him like a Japanese flower in water. (p. 103)

Tey sounds her theme of criminal vanity in every novel, but she

is not unique in her opinions. Agatha Christie, too, often has
Poirot comment on the pride and egotism of the criminal.

Grant arrives at Scoone with no symptoms of his claustrophobia, even though he had spent some time in the small cabin of
an airplane. Tommy meets him at the hotel and they drive home.
Grant discovers Zoë Kentallen is now visiting Laura and suspects
his cousin of some discreet matchmaking. He also discovers a
large bag of mail in answer to his ad. The woman and the letters
keep him totally occupied, too busy to give much thought to his
own health problems. He finds out nothing about the poem, but
does discover Zoë to be disconcertingly intriguing. In fact, he
even toys with the idea of resigning from the force and living in
the country on his independent income. Marriage, he thinks,
might even fit into the picture somewhere. This, incidentally, is
as close as Grant ever comes to the altar. In the classical
detective novel, the hero is never married, having only his
"Watson" as a companion and confidant in a muted, latent
homosexual relationship. One of S.S. Van Dine's unbreakable
rules insisted "No love interest."[2] Yet, since World War II,
detectives have married and occasionally functioned as an
investigative team. Nick and Nora Charles (Dashiell Hammett,
The Thin Man), Tommy and Tuppence Beresford (Agatha
Christie, *N or M?*), Rory and Troy Alleyn (Ngaio Marsh, *Final
Curtain*), and John and Judith Appleby (Michael Innes, *The
Crabtree Affair*) are some of the best known married investiga-
tors. Even Dorothy L. Sayers married off Lord Peter in *Busman's
Honeymoon*. Grant, however, remains unattached.

While fishing in a nearby stream, Grant's attention is caught by
Tad Cullen, a pilot for Oriental Commercial Airlines Ltd., who
has arrived to question Grant about his ad. Cullen insists that his
missing friend, Bill Kenrick, had once used those or very similar
words. Kenrick was to have met Cullen in Paris on leave, but he
never appeared and Cullen is frankly worried. Bill had been
flying a route in Arabia and had been caught in a sudden storm of
hurricane force. After that, "He seemed to me a bit—concussed,
if you get me" (p. 119). His behavior changed, he became more
quiet, even "cagey," and studied maps with what amounted to be
an obsession. Cullen has a picture of his friend and Grant
identifies Kenrick as the man on the train. Grant resolves to find
an answer to this conundrum.

The following day Grant journeys to Scoone's library once

again, this time to try to discover why Kenrick had been obsessed with the maps of Arabia. "If Grant had any last lingering doubt that the man in B-Seven was Bill Kenrick, it went when he found that the desert part of south-eastern Arabia, the Empty Quarter, was called the Rub'al-Khali" (p. 141). This is what sounded to Old Yoghourt as "Rob the Caley." Grant devotes his interest to the Empty Quarter and finds reference to monkeys, easily the "talking beasts" of the poem. He finds further reference to Wabar, the "Atlantis of Arabia" (p. 141).

Somewhere in the time between legend and history it had been destroyed by fire for its sins. For it had been rich and sinful beyond the power of words to express. . . . And now Wabar, the fabled city, was a cluster of ruins guarded by the shifting sands, by cliffs of stone that forever changed place and form; and inhabited by a monkey race and by evil jinns. (p. 141)

No one had ever found the ruins. Grant, always a careful scholar, discovers the name of the most famous authority on Arabia, Heron Lloyd. He immediately books two seats on a flight to London for himself and Cullen and returns to Laura's home. Grant is grateful to the dead Kenrick for giving him a puzzle and distraction that, he believes, helped cure him.

. . . Grant became aware that Bill Kenrick had done him a final service for which he had not yet had credit. Bill Kenrick has saved him from falling in love with Zoë Kentallen.
A few more hours would have done it. A few more hours in her uninterrupted company, and he would have been involved past recovery. (p. 146)

Cullen and Grant (now only vaguely plagued by his internal devil) return to London to continue the investigation. Grant visits Heron Lloyd. The man is vain and a "true Narcissus." This should suggest to the astute reader that Lloyd is a criminal and probably in some way responsible for Kenrick's death. The explorer does admit having met Kenrick, but insists he laughed at the tale of Wabar. Kenrick, he states, saw a meteor crater, and that was all.
While Tad searches for Bill Kenrick's London hotel, Grant puzzles on Lloyd.

What was familiar about Lloyd?

He went back in his mind over the few moments before his first feeling of recognition. What had Lloyd been doing? Pulling open the panel of the book cupboard. Pulling it open with a gesture self-consciously graceful, faintly exhibitionist. What was there in that to provoke a sense of familiarity?

And there was something even more curious.

Why had Lloyd said "On what?" when he had mentioned Kenrick's scribbling? (p. 178)

Suddenly Grant realizes that Heron Lloyd reminds him of Wee Archie. The similarity lies in their pathological vanity. "Vanity. The first requisite in wrong-going. The constant factor in the criminal mind" (p. 178).

Grant, now excited and stimulated by his investigation, persuades Lloyd's window washer to apprentice Tad for a day so that he can get into Lloyd's house legally and without suspicion. The Inspector then calls Marta Hallard, his actress acquaintance from previous novels. Her nephew, Rory, is in Arabia exploring with another famous expert, Kinsey-Hewitt. Lloyd refused to take Rory along, Marta assumes, because "he wants the whole stage" (p. 191). Finding himself at the inevitable temporary dead end, Grant advertises for Kenrick's luggage and goes to Marseilles to interview Charles Martin's family. Since Kenrick was carrying Martin's identity papers, there must be some connection. Yet he can discover none. Martin was "a bad boy" (p. 197), lazy, irresponsible, and headstrong, but a good mechanic.

That evening, Grant, disconsolate and distracted, notices briefly the newspaper headlines, including news of a plane crash in the Alps. But the following morning, the headlines totally capture his attention.

SHANGRI LA REALLY EXISTS. SENSATIONAL DISCOVERY. HISTORIC FIND IN ARABIA. (p. 205)

Kinsey-Hewitt, it seems, discovered Wabar in the Empty Quarter. Grant is furious. He is certain that Lloyd had murdered Kenrick so that he could locate Wabar and have the glory of the discovery. He determines to confront the explorer at once. But Lloyd is gone. Grant begins writing a statement for the Yard when he notices a letter on his desk. It is, neatly written, a complete confession by Lloyd. He had murdered Kenrick and arranged it to look like an accident. In all but her first novel, *The Man in the Queue* (1929), Tey's murders have been arranged to look accidental. This, of course, keeps them both neater, less gory, and generally bloodless in the best classical tradition of the Golden Age of mystery writing. It was Lloyd's plane that had crashed in the Alps, a combination of murder for the pilot and his companion, and suicide.

Although Grant did not solve the crime by detection, he insists that he could have. Lloyd's fingerprints covered Martin's papers and from that he might possibly have extracted a confession. Grant returns to the Yard with a report on the Kenrick murder and happily resumes his job, surprised that he ever thought of resignation and marriage.

II   *The Novel's Atmosphere*

Although some of Tey's previous novels, notably *Brat Farrar*, *The Franchise Affair*, and *To Love and Be Wise*, have intriguing and memorable settings, *The Singing Sands* unquestionably has the most significant and colorful atmosphere. "The background of the Scottish Highlands and the Hebrides is painted with magnificent color."[3] Even the descriptions of London, Paris, and Marseilles, no easy task as any travel writer would agree, are delightfully specific and unforgettable.

Marseilles, at close quarters was no jeweller's creation. It was the usual noisy crowded place filled with impatient taxi-horns and the smell of stale coffee; that very French smell that haunts its houses with the ghosts of ten million coffee brewings. But the sun shone, and the striped awnings flapped a little in the breeze from the Mediterranean, and the mimosa displayed its pale and expensive yellow in prodigal masses. As a companion picture to the grey and scarlet of London it was, he thought, perfect. (p. 196)

Comparing such descriptions with those in Tey's first novel, *The Man in the Queue,* the reader can note the development of the writer's craft:

Slowly he walked up the gaudy pavement towards Charing in and out of the changing light from the shop windows: rose light, gold light, diamond light; shoe shop, clothes shop, jewellers.[4]

III   *The Critics*

The Singing Sands could be termed both a novel of character and a travelogue. Traditionalists would no doubt balk slightly at the term detective novel. "As a detective story it has faults: an extremely slow start and an ending which, though ingenious, is reached rather by intuition than detection."[5] Furthermore, the emphasis lies not on detection so much as on the detective, his personal problems, obsessions, compulsions, and the methods he uses to deal with these. This is a tale long and leisurely and as rich in observation as its predecessors. It seems no exaggeration to say that although its mystery hangs upon a striking and exotic late discovery one is as much absorbed in Grant and in (say) the difficulty he has in discovering and then enduring any locally produced food in the Hebrides, or in his affectionate observation of his young cousin, Pat.[6]

Anthony Boucher terms *Singing Sands* "a study in detection as a method of psychotherapy."[7]

As writers and others know, the same work that breaks you down under pressure may be sheer relaxation when done for your own pleasure; Grant's mind will not leave the case alone, and in its eventual solution he finds his own rehabilitation. (p. 59)

Most critics agree that the mystery is negligible, but the characterization and settings are vividly memorable and significant.

IV   *Grant's Central Position*

Inspector Grant, then, is the key to the novel. Although he has been compulsive and obsessive from the first, his nerves have at long last given way to a combination of external and internal pressure. Amazingly, he escapes an ulcer, but succumbs to "a case of nerves" or a breakdown. His character as presented in Tey's previous novels points relentlessly to some inevitable "breaking."

"It came from four years of consistent overwork and an overgrown conscience. You always were a demon where conscience was concerned. Quite tiresome you could be. Would you rather have a spot of claustrophobia or a stroke?" (p. 49)

Several elements combine to bring about his collapse. First, his terrier-like stubbornness. "Nothing has ever made you deviate by a hair's breadth from any line that you once set your mind on. You've always been a damned Juggernaut" (p. 152). Second, of course, is his nagging conscience, the "voice" that always argues with him. Third, Grant lacks any emotional involvement in wife, family, or mistress to distract his mind from work. The reason, according to him, is his job. "With leisure there would be time to share his life. Time to love and be loved" (p. 114). This seems so much nonsense to most people who manage both jobs and family. The reader might further be reminded that Grant has an independent income and no need to work at all. In this light, then, his overwork clearly appears as an obsession. Finally, there is his pride, vanity perhaps so akin to the inevitable criminal vanity of which Tey often writes. The Inspector cannot allow a question to go unanswered and relies on and is tremendously proud of his "flair":

The Commissioner had once said to him: "You have the most priceless of all attributes for your job, and that is flair. But don't let it ride you, Grant. Don't let your imagination take hold. Keep it your servant." (p. 193)

Needless to say, Grant rarely if ever followed this advice.

Grant carries on an inner dialogue, providing internally, so to speak, his own Watson. Tey uses this technique in dealing with other obsessed central characters, Brat Farrar, and Lucy Pym, for example. Ironically, Grant personally identifies with the dead man. Symbolically he himself is dead initially, incapable of responding rationally, unable to cope with his job or individuals. Yet he is reborn, as it were, through the death of Bill Kenrick. He is intrigued, taken out of himself, and in the course of investigation experiences the reawakening of self-control and normality. It must be remembered that Tey was dying as she wrote this novel and was undoubtedly expressing a personal desire for rejuvenation and rebirth. She clearly recognizes the ability of the mind to make the body ill.

V   *The Minor Characters*

While Grant's illness and responses direct the action, the minor characters are delightfully realistic and memorable. The description of Old Yoghourt, for example, is succinct and detailed although brief.

For twenty years Murdo Gallacher had done the absolute minimum. He had been bored by the job before he had been a week at it, but he had found it a rich lode and he had stayed to mine it. If you got morning tea from Murdo, the tea would be week, the biscuit soft, the sugar dirty, the tray slopped and the spoon missing; but when Murdo came to collect the tray the protests which you had been rehearsing died on your lips. Now and then an Admiral of the Fleet or something like that would venture an opinion that it was damned awful tea, but the ruck smiled and paid up. For twenty years they had paid up, weary and browbeaten and blackmailed. And Murdo had collected. (p. 6)

Interestingly, women play a less significant part in *The Singing Sands* than in any previous novel. Laura, like a plump pillow, momentarily comforts her cousin; Zoë momentarily intrigues him, and Marta momentarily feeds him. All, having done their duty as women, retreat quickly to the background. In terms of the structural action, they are totally insignificant. In terms of Grant's problems and personalities, they are brief, but masculine and reassuring episodes.

Finally, among the characters, are the victim (never seen alive), his friend, and his murderer. The victim, a trifle odd and surely a bit unsophisticated, serves to lure Grant back to normalcy. His friend, Tad Cullen, takes the place of Simpson or Williams, Grant's underlings on the force. All are treated with kindness, tolerance, and a small smattering of condescension. On the whole, they are not very interesting.

VI   *The Character of the Murderer*

Of all Tey's murderers, Heron Lloyd is by far the most intriguing. His home reveals his soul.

The interior of the house, too, had the Arab bareness and space without any suggestion that a piece of the East had been transported to London. Beyond the figure of the manservant who answered his ring, he could see the clean walls and rich carpet; an idiom adapted, not a decor transposed. (p. 161)

And he has the personality and looks of a Valentino.

Lloyd was the Arab of the desert idealised to the nth. He was, Grant thought with amusement, the Arab of the circulating libraries. It was across the saddle of Arabs like Heron Lloyd that blameless matrons in the Crescents and Drives and Avenues had been carried off to a fate worse then death. (p. 162)

And finally, Lloyd has the fatal flaw that ensures his downfall—vanity.

VII   *The Novel's Poetry*

At least part of Grant's obsession centers around the odd verse scribbled by Kenrick on a newspaper:

> The beasts that talk,
> The streams that stand,
> The stones that walk,
> The singing sands
> . . . .
> . . . .
> That guard the way
> to Paradise. . .(p. 13)

Once again Tey's wry humor focuses on her detective. Assuming such a place is only in Scotland, Grant is reinforced by Wee Archie whose nationalism merges into extreme radicalism and anarchy. The Inspector can make the Hebrides fit such a description with only a little stretching. Actually Kenrick was writing of his own paradise in Arabia, although Grant interprets it as applying to his paradise in Scotland. In an extremely subtle way, it may be suspected that Tey is blasting critics who insist theirs is the only correct interpretation of poem or play. Furthermore, it is curious that Grant, almost in spite of himself, has a poetic heart. In *To Love and Be Wise* he quoted verses; here he is enthralled with them and ultimately, of course, they point to his mental salvation. Doubtless Tey herself read and wrote poems. She probably felt them so self-revealing, however, that they have never been published and were perhaps destroyed.

VIII   *Reference to Nature*

Again as in *The Man in the Queue, A Shilling for Candles,* and *To Love and Be Wise,* the author has frequent references to rivers, streams, and oceans. In *The Singing Sands* as well as in the previous works, they prove a cleansing and purifying experience. Grant's problems are eased as he fishes with Pat and he feels reborn after a brief walk beside the Atlantic Ocean.

Grant's journey "home" to Scotland and what small family he has aids remarkably in his rehabilitation. It is as if the author were insisting, *au contraire* Thomas Wolfe, "You can go home again. It will be different, but it will refresh and renew you physically and spiritually." Tey herself seldom left Scotland.

IX   *Symbols*

Tey's system of interlocking symbols, complex and undoubtedly subconscious, suggest the leanings of a poet. The ruins that inspired Kenrick's verse reflect the ruins of Grant's mind and soul. It is only by rediscovering the site of past beauty and future intellectual promise that Grant is saved—and Kenrick, too, is immortalized. When Tey wrote *The Singing Sands* she undoubtedly knew of her approaching death. Thus did she reflect a desire for immortality of mind, if not body. She openly hoped her plays would grant her fame; instead, her so-called yearly knitting is the source of it.

X   *Themes*

In her final novel, Tey reunites her various themes. She again sees America as a land of challenge producing strong "tall, lean, tough, nasal, drawling, skeptical and indestructible" individuals (p. 199).

She reiterates her theories regarding criminal vanity:

It is a frightening thing because it is incurable. You can never convince Vanity that anyone else is of the slightest importance; he just doesn't understand what you are talking about. He will kill a person rather than

be put to the inconvenience of doing a six months' stretch. . . .
Criminals. . . . have one invariable characteristic: their pathological
vanity. (p. 182)

Again, she deals with the appearance-as-illusion theme.
Yoghourt assumes Kenrick only drunk, not dead, since the
compartment smells of alcohol. Later, the great and famous
explorer proves to be merely a vain criminal. She repeats the "in
place of another" theme with Kenrick first identified as Martin.
Finally, perhaps because of her impending death, she is
concerned with both paradise, in the lost city, and hell.

Hell wasn't a nice cosy place where you fried. Hell was a great cold
echoing cave where there was neither past nor future; a black echoing
desolation. Hell was concentrated essence of a winter morning after a
sleepless night of self-distaste. (p. 10)

XI *Links with Tey's First Novel*

There is no doubt that Tey's last novel closely resembled her
first, suggesting perhaps that *The Man the Queue* was ahead of its
time. Or perhaps, as the author herself was the first to admit, she
lacked original ideas. The novels, for example, are similar in
structure. Both begin with the death of an unknown man. In *The
Man in the Queue* the fact of murder is immediately obvious. In
The Singing Sands the discovery is slightly delayed. In both,
Grant investigates. The victim is never seen living and is hard to
trace. The victim, like the detective, was stubborn, determined,
and even compulsive. In both novels, Grant journeys to Scotland
where he inevitably fishes and is involved in a journey by water
and subsequently experiences rebirth of mind and attitude. In
both, the murderer is finally discovered only by a full confession.
The motive for murder is similar, too, protection of the
murderer's interests. In both, the Inspector is more or less on his
own in terms of investigation and cannot let go of the case until it
is solved to his satisfaction. The Yard, in both cases, is supremely
uninterested and remote.

   The Singing Sands, however, is a much more satisfying novel.
Tey was more accomplished at her craft and there is no doubt
that her descriptive abilities and character portraiture improved
in the maturation process.

CHAPTER 12

Conclusions

O F all of Elizabeth Mackintosh's work, only the eight mystery novels remain available to the general public at this time. Although the author herself would have deplored the situation, there is no doubt that the "Tey" novels are regarded as her most significant contribution to literature. The reasons are obvious. Drama has seldom been regarded as popular reading material, while the three Daviot novels and one biography have joined the thousands of forgotten volumes on library shelves, relegated to obscurity by the latest best seller. Detective and mystery fiction, however, remains popular.

Always a haven for scholars, the genre counts among its own such illustrious names as Dorothy L. Sayers, Cecil Day-Lewis, Willard Huntington Wright, and J.I.M. Stewart. Professional authors such as Raymond Chandler, Dashiell Hammett, Rex Stout, and Agatha Christie have added to the scholarly emphasis on style, a sense of human frailty and confusion in an often terrifying world. There is, nonetheless, in all detective fiction an unfailing sense of order; in spite of acts of violence, murder, and mayhem, the guilty are invariably punished while the good are rewarded. This explains both the appeal of the genre as well as its popularity. Scott Sutherland insists "Detective fiction which has . . . few close links with the everyday world . . . probably reflects current events, hopes and aspirations less than almost any other related medium."[1]

I *The Form*

In detective fiction, there are several basic patterns upon which endless variations are played. Roughly combined, they could be outlined as follows:

1) Murder;

2) Suspects identified, with detection taking place;
3) Introduction of clues and false trails;
4) An impasse and reversal of fortune for the detective;
5) Denouement: confrontation between criminal and detective;
6) Murderer is arrested or dies;
7) Explanation by the detective.

Each author, then, develops an individual "formula" using all or parts of the above outline as a method of structuring the novel. Some writers, like Dorothy L. Sayers and Josephine Tey, prefer to vary their formulas occasionally, while others prefer to rewrite essentially the same novel in different terms.

Tey's first two novels are examples of this latter approach. *The Man in the Queue* and *A Shilling for Candles* begin with what Sutherland terms the "Method of Sudden Plunge" or the body on the doorstep.[2] An unidentified corpse is discovered in a commonplace setting—a line in front of a theater waiting for tickets or a beach. Grant is then called in to solve the crime. Circumstantial evidence points irrefutably at one individual who then attempts to escape. Grant tracks down the suspected culprit who is by this point ill in some way.

A young ingenue, however, has faith that the suspect is innocent and causes Grant to question his own beliefs. After some deep soul searching, the Inspector follows more leads and ultimately is presented with or captures the real culprit, a woman with an obsession. Mrs. Wallis in *The Man in the Queue* wants to save her daughter, and Lydia Keats in *A Shilling for Candles* wants fame and fortune for herself.

Tey's third novel, *Miss Pym Disposes,* was published eleven years after the second, and shows significant changes in structure. Although, as in the first novels, the victim is somewhat unpleasant, and the wrong person is suspected, *Miss Pym Disposes* concentrates more on character than crime. It is as Sutherland prefers to term it, "the method of calculated approach." Most of the novel is spent in establishing individual traits, tendencies, and relationships, with the crime occurring late in the novel. Tey carefully builds up suspense with hints and foreshadowing.

In *The Franchise Affair* (1949), Tey combines the two of the above types of structure. The novel opens with the "body on the doorstep" so to speak, as Marion Sharpe and her mother are accused of kidnapping and beating a young girl. Suspense, dread, and fear are built up slowly and painstakingly until the final denouement in the courtroom when Betty Kane is "stripped" publicly and exposed as a trollop and liar.

In *Brat Farrar*, also published in 1949, Tey again portrays no actual murder in the novel. This approach is true, in fact, of both *To Love and Be Wise* (1950) and *The Daughter of Time* (1951), the two following works. *Brat Farrar*, like *To Love and Be Wise*, is more a novel of character than of crime. Initially involved in a plot to defraud the Ashbys, Farrar discovers both himself and the murderer of his look-alike, Patrick. Again, as in *Miss Pym Disposes*, there is a death which is, in theory at least, accidental. *To Love and Be Wise* is also a novel of fraud, dealing with a transvestite determined on murder. Again as in *Brat Farrar*, no murder occurs. The novel is mainly concerned with the effects of suspected murder on a small community of artists.

The Daughter of Time breaks both precedent and tradition. There is no action and no chase; the murderer as well as his victims have been dead for centuries. However, there is intensive, detailed, painstaking detection and investigation. Tey uses the traditional techniques of the investigator and applies them to history, using letters, sermons, diaries, and the like as evidence rather than live testimony. The approaches of detective and historian in the search for truth are similar indeed, as Tey indicates.

The Singing Sands, Tey's last detective novel published in 1952, returns in some respects to the basic formula used in *The Man in the Queue* and *A Shilling for Candles*. Again the body is on the doorstep, this time of a tired and worn Inspector who is on vacation. Initially planned to look like an accident, the murder is a carefully contrived affair. Grant's approach involves establishing the identity of the corpse as well as healing his own psyche. Once this has been accomplished, the identification of the murderer follows quickly and easily.

In all Tey's detective novels there is an abundance of false leads, hopes, and inferences. In six of the eight novels, the "hares and hounds" approach is used. The detective must at least try to trap the criminal. Only in *The Franchise Affair* and *Brat Farrar* is the criminal easily recognized by the reader at the outset. The detectives agonize painfully over their moral responsibilities and inevitably reach an impasse. Then, suddenly and often by coincidence or accident, the detective is aware of the solution. Explanations, when necessary, are blessedly brief and to the point, unlike those lectures by Dr. Fell (John Dickson Carr) or Hercule Poirot (Agatha Christie). In all but the final novel, *The Singing Sands,* an innocent person appears guilty of a crime of some sort or suffers for it. Ironically, in *Brat Farrar,* the detective too is a suffering criminal who is also later forgiven and loved. Tey's settings vary somewhat from novel to novel. She includes places such as a school, horse farm, small town and hospital in or near London or Scotland.

II *The Victims*

In Tey's work as in most mystery and detective novels, the victims are sometimes living, sometimes dead. The living victims arouse some sympathy in the reader, while the dead are either unloved or seem remote.

The living victims in Tey's first four novels, *The Man in the Queue, A Shilling for Candles, Miss Pym Disposes,* and *The Franchise Affair,* are the suspects as well as the detectives. Lamont, the "Levantine" who roomed with Sorrel, the dead victim, runs from Grant; he is living an existence of fear, self-loathing, and anxiety. When captured, he suffers a concussion and nearly drowns. Tisdall, in *A Shilling for Candles,* is another suspect, ironically a temporary "roomer" with the dead Christine Clay. He too runs away. His name, however, is cleared before he is found suffering from exposure and possible pneumonia. In these first two novels, Grant, too, in some ways falls a victim both to his own erroneous conclusions and to his "other self" which tortures him with doubts and accusations of incompetence.

In *Miss Pym Disposes,* the living victim is Innes who will spend her life "atoning" for the death of Rouse. Lucy Pym, the halfhearted detective, suffers too. At the mercy of her other self, she agonizes over decisions, allowing her merciful self to triumph over her moral self.

The two living victims of the fraud in *The Franchise Affair* are Marion Sharpe and her mother. They are ostracized and their property is destroyed because the townspeople believe the lies of Betty Kane. Their lawyer, Robert Blair, becomes the detec-

tive, determined to expose the lies of the young girl. He becomes
emotionally involved with Marion and suffers feelings of futility,
both in his relationship with her and his attempts to solve the
case.

In *Brat Farrar* also, multiple victims appear. Everyone,
particularly Aunt Bee, had suffered from guilt over Patrick's
supposed suicide, with the exception of his twin, Simon, who had
in fact murdered the boy. The family suffers too when Simon is
killed and Brat seriously injured. Brat himself must endure the
barbs of conscience he feels initially at imposing on the Ashbys.
Later, he must determine whether or not to expose Patrick's
murderer and hurt the family still more; the revelation ultimately occurs by accident.

To Love and Be Wise, again a novel of fraud, is in fact a story of
victims. Even the perpetrator of the fraud, Leslie Searle, was a
victim of the lies and charms of her cousin, Marguerite. Walter
Whitmore, the self-centered radio commentator, suffers under
the cloud of suspected murder. His fiancée Liz suffers from
extremely mixed emotions, not knowing why or exactly how she
responds to Searle and yet feeling a loyalty toward Walter. Her
mother, Emma Garrowby, suffers from Searle's mere existence,
fearing it will destroy the long-hoped-for liaison between her
daughter and Walter. By the end of the novel, the guilt feelings
of all those victims have been purged.

In Tey's last two novels, *The Daughter of Time* and *The Singing
Sands,* there are no living victims. True, Inspector Grant does
endure pain in both, physical as well as psychological, but this is
brought about by his job rather than the present case. In fact,
both puzzles—that of Richard III and of the dead man in B-
Seven—help Grant to recover his emotional balance and
stability.

Tey's dead victims are generally odd, perhaps a bit mad, liked
by very few, and occasionally distant. In *The Man in the Queue*
and *A Shilling for Candles* the deceased is admired and liked
only by the major suspect. Neither Bert Sorrell nor Christine
Clay are seen alive in the novels. *Miss Pym Disposes* breaks the
formula by leaving Rouse very much alive throughout most of
the novel. She is also very much unloved and, if Lucy Pym's
deductions about the cheating notes are correct, Rouse is not a
very admirable character. In *The Franchise Affair* and *To Love
and Be Wise* the victims are all living, while in *Brat Farrar* the

murder occurs many years before the action of the novel begins. The victim can be remembered only vaguely as being "nice." The distance is even greater in *The Daughter of Time* since all the participants are long dead. The princes do not emerge as characters at all, although they were in fact the victims of murder. Only Richard remains significant, damned by lies and prevarications in his lifetime and painted by Henry VII as a deformed murderer.

In *The Singing Sands*, Tey once again returns to the basic formula. The murder occurs just before the action begins and, as in *A Shilling for Candles* and *Miss Pym Disposes*, appears at first to be an accident. The dead man, however, is the most likable of all Tey's victims—a trifle naive surely, but sincere and kind. Most of the victims in Tey's novels suffer from some sort of obsession. Sorrell wished to murder Ray Marcable in *The Man in the Queue* and then kill himself; Christine Clay continually picked up strangers in *A Shilling for Candles*, hid her own identity, and preferred to communicate with them rather than with friends. Richard III was obsessed with being a fair and honest king, insisting on trusting the Woodvilles who plotted against him if the author is correct. Bill Kenrick in *The Singing Sands* was determined to return to his Shangri-la in the desert and take the credit for its discovery.

III   The Criminals

Ironically, the murderers and criminals are also obsessed, most with personal gain, while two appear to be concerned with helping a loved one. Lydia Keats, Betty Kane, Simon Ashby, and Brat Farrar, as well as Leslie Searle, Henry VII, and Heron Lloyd all commit crimes to protect themselves or their interests. Lydia, Betty, Henry VII, and Lloyd act to protect their reputation while Simon and Brat primarily consider their personal gain. Searle is the only character acting from a motive of revenge and, perhaps because she does not execute her crime, or perhaps because of her own personal confusion, she is a sympathetic character. Mrs. Wallis, who does murder to protect the life of her daughter, is also well regarded, even by Inspector Grant. Her motive apparently clears her of responsibility for the crime. However, Nash, who acts to obtain a post for her best friend Innes, is treated with extreme ambivalence: "She wondered why she had never

noticed before how cold those blue eyes were. Brilliant and cold
and shallow."[4] And yet, Lucy Pym basically liked Nash.

Tey had a firm belief that all criminals were vain and egotistic.
The murderer or criminal has a demonic pride as well as an
overblown ego. He cannot and will not suffer for any crimes
committed. The murderer may go mad like Lydia Keats or
commit suicide like Heron Lloyd, but his only regret, apparently,
is being caught. Tey would insist that this is true of the "criminal
class" as a whole.

IV   The Detectives

Tey stood at the crossroads of detective fiction. On the one
hand, beginning in the Golden Age was the gentleman detective—erudite, clever, wealthy, with a fine palate and a deep
sense of decency. Sometimes married, always with faithful
friend or valet or both, the detective was witty, sensitive, and
heroic. On the other hand was the "hard boiled dick"
detective, developed by Hammet and Chandler initially, and
continued by Ross Macdonald and John D. Macdonald among
others. Chandler defines the qualities of his detective in *The
Simple Art of Murder*. The detective cannot be mean, "neither
tarnished nor afraid":

He must be a complete man and a common man and yet an unusual man.
He must be, to use a rather weathered phrase, a man of honor . . .
I think he might seduce a duchess and I am quite sure he would not
spoil a virgin; if he is a man of honor in one thing, he is that in all things.
    He is a relatively poor man . . . He is a common man . . . He will
take no man's money dishonestly and no man's insolence without due
and dispassionate revenge. He is a lonely man and his pride is that you
will treat him as a proud man.[5]

Finally, the "hard boiled dick" has "a rude wit, a lively sense of
the grotesque, a disgust for sham, and a contempt for pettiness."[7]
Inspector Grant, then, has qualities of both detectives. He is a
gentleman, educated, with an independent income, fine palate
(as he assures us in *To Love and Be Wise*), and with a sort of dour
Scottish decency about him. He is surely lonely and proud,
though it is doubtful that he would even consider seducing a
duchess. Nor would he consider revenge his forte, but he cannot

tolerate pettiness (as evidenced by his emotional reaction to Wee Archie in *The Singing Sands*). He searches for hidden truths with his fellow detectives on both sides of the road, Peter Wimsey and Sam Spade.

Yet Grant has one quality that distinguishes him from other detectives, makes him, in fact, fairly unique. That is his nagging, torturing "other self": his conscience. It is this which nearly drives him to mental breakdown, and no wonder. Proud of his flair, he worries a case like a terrier at a rat hole. This torture is self-inflicted by all Tey's detectives—Miss Pym, Brat Farrar, and Inspector Grant. Only Robert Blair, the somewhat naive lawyer in *The Franchise Affair*, escapes the agony of too closely thinking on the event. All enjoy overdeveloped consciences and are bitterly self-critical (except Blair). Each has a dialogue with the "other self"—one self insisting on morality and justice, the other arguing for kindness, self-interest, and avoiding unpleasantness. Each detective is crammed full of good intentions which often go astray. They are deeply dedicated to their particular line of work, and most have some funds to relieve them of the mundane everyday budget problems. While Inspector Grant is the symbol for Scotland Yard, Miss Pym is the embodiment of the spinster detective. Though scarcely professional as is Miss Silver (Patricia Wentworth), she nonetheless becomes unwittingly involved in crime. Brat Farrar is the criminal-turned-detective, a type popular presently in film and television. Robert Blair, finally, is the lawyer detective, a type made most familiar by Erle Stanley Gardner (Perry Mason) and Sara Woods (Anthony Maitland). All share the same traits of honesty, sincerity, loneliness, sensitivity, and occasional foolishness—traits which Tey must have seen somewhere in herself.

V   *The Good, the Bad, and the In Between*

The women portrayed by Tey can generally be classified into four categories, three of them "good" and one "bad." First, among the "good" women is the aunt or mother figure. This, it seems, is one of Tey's favorites since the type appears in the Daviot dramas as well as in the mystery novels. To this woman, life centers solely around a man or men. It is her duty, as she sees it, to devote herself to satisfying her male's every whim, even and preferably before he is aware of it himself. She worries about her charges—which often include girls—and has a simple faith that truth will out and all will be right eventually. Sometimes she can be hard and cruel in support of the weak and ineffectual male: at other times she is soft, sensitive, and intuitive. Among these motherly types are Mary (*Kif*), Mrs. Everett (*Man in the Queue*), Sara Ellis (*Expensive Halo*), Miss Pym (*Miss Pym Disposes*), Aunt Lin (*The Franchise Affair*), Aunt Bee (*Brat Farrar*), Lavinia Fitch, Marta Hallard, and Emma Garrowby (*To Love and Be Wise*), Laura (*The Singing Sands*), and Elizabeth (*The Privateer*).

Tey's second type could be called the young ingenue. This character, apparently one of her favorites until *The Franchise Affair* was written, appears with frequency and regularity in the mystery novels. The ingenue is clever, witty, kind, generous, sensitive, intuitive where men often are not. She is often outspoken and always correct in her character evaluations. Miss Dinmont in *The Man in the Queue* is the first example of the ingenue, followed by Erica (*A Shilling for Candles*), Desterro (*Miss Pym Disposes*), and the twins, Jane and Ruth (*Brat Farrar*). In *The Franchise Affair,* the ingenue becomes abruptly one of the "bad" women in Tey and does not reappear in her novels.

The third and last type of "good" woman might be called the "unwomanly woman." First seen in Henrietta in *Miss Pym Disposes,* this type is free from any male domination and always will be. She is independent, often outspoken, aware of her responsibilities as well as her physical and emotional drawbacks. Most surprisingly, she is content with her life, a comment that cannot always be made even of Inspector Grant. Marion in *The Franchise Affair* is the best example in Tey's work of the "unwomanly woman." This character does occur again in an interesting variation as Leslie Searle in *The Singing Sands.* Searle, though possessing two identities, is nonetheless self-confident, independent, and deeply aware of the problems of others.

The final type is the "bad" woman. She is selfish and unprincipled, but clever and often extremely talented. It is sometimes difficult to recognize a "bad" woman because initially, at least, she appears attractive and likable. This character type does not appear in the later novels *To Love and Be Wise* and *The Daughter of Time* where the dividing lines between good and evil often become a bit blurred. Ray Marcable, the actress who skillfully upstages her leading man in *The Man in the Queue,* is a modified version of the bad woman. Lydia Keats, the murderer in *A Shilling for Candles,* is a perfect example, along with Beau Nash (*Miss Pym Disposes*) and Betty Kane (*The Franchise Affair*). Ironically, the bad woman in *The Singing Sands,* Zoë Kentallen, is bad only because of her attraction for Grant, which makes her extremely dangerous. Needless to say, the Inspector deftly overcomes temptation and returns to his own true love, his job at Scotland Yard.

Tey's "good" men are generally the same type. They are men of some authority—inspectors, policemen, chief constables, lawyers, or vicars—faithful in good times and bad. Sometimes, as in the cases of Richard III, Claverhouse, Harry Morgan, they appear at first to be villainous and cruel. However, once the author explains the "true" facts—that is, her theories of history and character—the villain becomes a hero. Richard III was a good and faithful king, Claverhouse a clever and diplomatic soldier, and Harry Morgan a talented sailor defending his country against the evil Spanish.

A second type of male character often appearing in Tey's novels and dramas is that of the "weak" man. He is sometimes vain, always foolish, and inevitably becomes involved in awkward and occasionally dangerous situations. Lamont, for example, the "Levantine" in *The Man in the Queue,* panics when he thinks Grant suspects him, and runs away, further arousing the Inspector's doubts. Lamont's ultimate capture results in near death. Tisdall in *A Shilling for Candles* is equally foolish in his actions with much the same results. In *Miss Pym Disposes,* the weak man plays a very small part as Edward Adrian, the actor who dotes on the adoration of young girls but cannot persuade Catherine Lux of whom he is fond to go to dinner. Gareth Ellis in Tey's non-detective novel *Expensive Halo* is another weak man; naive and uncomplicated, he falls in love with a society girl. Only his sister Mary saves him from the inevitable ruin of a permanent alliance with Ursula Deane.

Brat Farrar is, initially at least, one of Tey's weak men. He allows himself to be used in an effort to defraud the Ashby family. Like the others of this type, he knows what he should do but chooses instead the easier, less frightening way. For Brat, it was easier to defraud the family than to starve in London, just as it was easier for Lamont and Tisdall to run away. The last insecure and foolish young man to appear in Tey's novels in Walter Whitmore in *To Love and Be Wise*. Walter's disgusting vanity is only a thin shell hiding his tender and sensitive ego

The truly bad men in Tey's novels are those for whom there is no redemption. They are, it seems, evil through and through, unprincipled, amoral, and vice-ridden, though often assuming a disguise of pious certitude. Brother Aloysius, for example, in *A Shilling for Candles*, assumes the attitude of quiet asceticism while at the same time he and his mistress are planning to decamp with the monastic funds. Another especially hateful character is Alfred Ellis in *Expensive Halo*, the psalm-singing, thieving greengrocer. Simon in *Brat Farrar* and Henry VII in *The Daughter of Time* are further examples of the "bad" man. Surprisingly, the largest number of these disreputable characters appear in *The Singing Sands*, Tey's posthumous novel. Heron Lloyd is the unprincipled explorer who will kill to get fame and glory, for example. "Old Yoghourt," the ill-tempered, nasty porter, appears in the first chapter and throughout the novel. Wee Archie reappears, "The vain, vicious little bastard,"[8] as Grant calls him. In *Claverhouse* and *The Privateer*, both works based on historical research, evil comes in groups. In *Claverhouse* it is the "Covenanters," "the Kirk," whose ministers preach sedition, rebellion, and murder, while in *The Privateer*, the villains are the Spanish who torture, rape, maim, and thieve with wild abandon.

Of these three types, it would seem that Tey generally preferred the "weak" man. Tisdall, Lamont, and Walter, for example, are treated with sympathy and understanding and are developed most completely as individual characters. She had little patience with hypocrites and unprincipled characters, portraying them with no significantly redeeming characteristics. Of the good men, only Inspector Grant and Robert Blair (*The Franchise Affair*) emerge as realistic individuals whose emotions, actions, and reactions are displayed in detail.

VI   *Tey's Symbolic World*

Tey uses two types of symbols in her novels, psychological and physical. The psychological symbols hinge primarily upon a character's behavior and motives and generally betray the deepest emotions of the individual. Searle's "oddness," for example, is taken by all who met her in *To Love and Be Wise* as something enthralling and dangerous, and indicates her lack of sexual identity. Simon's quicksilver temper and egotistic attitudes in *Brat Farrar* betray his murderous tendencies. The same may be said for Lydia Keats (*A Shilling for Candles*). Nash's easy self-confident determination and clear blue eyes in *Miss Pym* reflect an empty, amoral soul.

Tey's physical symbols are ordinarily used quite ironically. For example, the candles in *A Shilling for Candles* suggest a religious piety, a certain holiness. Yet the shilling for candles is given to the confidence man, Brother Aloysius, Christine Clay's amoral brother. The vacuum, or "The Abhorrence," as it was called in *Miss Pym Disposes*, both cleans the gym and reflects the vacuum in which the girls are living—the unreal atmosphere in which murder can occur. In *The Singing Sands*, too, the newspaper on which Kenrick writes his poem was meant originally as a method of communication. Ironically, the poem Kenrick communicates to Grant causes the Inspector first to heal his own mental wounds and later to discover Kenrick's identity and murderer. In the same manner, Patrick's unique pencil in *Brat Farrar* identifies his decomposed body and points to the killer.

Tey uses many ironic clothing symbols. The overcoat, in *A Shilling for Candles*, for example, was originally meant for protection. However, it exposes and betrays Tisdall who is suspected of the murder and Lydia Keats who actually accomplished the crime. The lipstick, symbol of adult femininity, betrays Betty Kane in *The Franchise Affair*, just as the lipstick and shoes betray Leslie Searle in *To Love and Be Wise*.

Of the author's use of rivers and journeys, much has already been said. Grant often embarks on a journey or quest for truth. This he ultimately finds, but always in an unexpected and surprising manner. Rivers and oceans have a deleterious or a cleansing effect. They can be used for accident or murder; yet whenever Inspector Grant becomes immersed, either physically or metaphorically, he emerges renewed and refreshed. Inevitably, his immersion usually suggests that he is about to discover the answer to the problem which has been tormenting him.

Finally, most of Tey's settings are symbolic of a closed, well-regulated environment. Scotland Yard, small villages, horse farms, schools, hospitals, are all withdrawn, isolated, separate, and unique. Crimes may occur, but a solution is inevitable in such a small world. This must have been reassuring to both the author and her readers in the postwar, unreliable, unpredictable world.

VII *The Themes*

Tey, like most authors, reiterates a limited number of themes in her novels. The most pervading of all is that of deception—things are not what they seem. Appearances are deceiving, the author feels. A man who looks guilty is in fact innocent, while an innocent-appearing person is guilty. Individuals seem to be what they are not; Brat Farrar seems to be the long missing and presumed dead Patrick Ashby while Leslie Searle appears as a strikingly handsome man when she is in fact a woman. No one is as reliable as they seem. The ever-faithful Liz Garrowby could be lured away from her fiancé Walter by Searle. Those who make a big display of religion are especially untrustworthy. Albert Ellis, for example, in *Expensive Halo* is a part-time preacher, full-time Bible quoter and thief. The world must have seemed an extremely deceptive place to the author.

A second theme frequently occurring in the Tey novels is that of mistaken identity or "in place of another." Kenrick in *The Singing Sands* is at first identified as Charles Martin, a Frenchman. Brat Farrar and Leslie Searle impersonate non-living individuals. Brat, as the result of Simon's death, ultimately replaces him in the family's affections. In this novel too, Aunt Bee replaces the mother for Brat and Uncle Charles replaces Brat's unreliable father, Walter.

Thirdly, most of the characters are unable to form significant relationships. Most are isolated due to their chronic inability to respond freely. When Grant himself is tempted to fall in love with Zoë Kentallen in *The Singing Sands,* he is at first frightened and then deeply relieved when his job calls him away from her siren song. He never feels threatened by Marta Hallard, for whom acting supersedes personal emotion. The author herself tended to be remote and distant, having few if any friends and no one close to her. Only in *The Privateer,* her last novel, are close friends portrayed. Here Harry Morgan is seen as willing to lose his own life to protect or avenge a friend. Since Tey spent her last year of life dying painfully alone, the reader might see this as a mute protest against an empty existence.

In her mystery and detection novels, Tey deals with a number of minor themes, including the total depravity of the criminal.

Your true criminal . . . has two unvarying characteristics, and it is these two characteristics which make him a criminal. Monstrous vanity and colossal selfishness. And they are both as integral, as ineradicable as the texture of the skin. You might as well talk of "reforming" the colour of one's eyes.[8]

Furthermore, as Marion insists in *The Franchise Affair* and Grant believes in *The Daughter of Time,* a person's characteristics can be recognized in his face and handwriting. The color of Kane's eyes, for example, betrays her as a trollop, while Richard III's face indicates suffering, not villainy, a face belonging on the bench, not in the dock. The depravity of criminals can be blamed on several things. First, the author would insist, is heredity. In *The Man in the Queue* Grant states: "His grandmother had been Italian, and if he hadn't inherited the knife he had probably inherited the will to use one . . ."[9] And later in *The Franchise Affair:*

Even the Bishop of Larborough would find some difficulty in thinking up a case for her. Her usual "environment" hobby-horse is no good this time. Betty Kane had everything that he recommends for the cure of the criminal: love, freedom to develop her talents, education, security. It's quite a poser for his lordship when you come to consider it, because he doesn't believe in heredity. He thinks that criminals are made, and therefore can be unmade. "Bad blood" is just an old superstition, in the Bishop's estimation.[10]

Furthermore, "with prison no more penitential than a not very good public school, and the death sentence on the point of being abolished"[11] there is little to discourage the criminal. The press aids and abets by being "soft" on the criminals, as pointed out in both *The Franchise Affair* and *To Love and Be Wise.*

In her mystery novels Tey portrays America as a land of challenge; cruel, harsh, demanding productive work of its residents, it is still somehow fascinating. The land produces "tall, lean, though nasal, drawling, skeptical and indestructible" individuals.[12] Carradine in *The Daughter of Time* must present his father with a book as proof of his labors and Tisdall is bequeathed a ranch in California which, it is presumed, will "make a man of him."

Kif, Claverhouse, and *The Privateer,* three of the Daviot non-detective works, deal with the theme of the "honest rogue." Daviot insists that appearances may lead the public to believe these men were thieves or murderers. In fact, they were victims of circumstance acting from the best of motives. Richard III in both the play and the Tey novel is also presented in this light. If Tey saw appearances as deceiving in real life, it was also true of history, she postulated.

If the reader were to make judgments regarding the author's philosophy by reading her works, some conclusions could be stated with certainty. Elizabeth Mackintosh was a conservative woman as are most writers of detective fiction. She was strongly in favor of a hard-nosed approach to law and order and felt, like some elected officials, that the press often hindered investigative work in government and was indeed "soft" on criminals. That she herself gave no personal interviews indicates the strength of her feelings. She had a deep distrust of blatantly religious individuals, fearing that they, like so many other aspects of life, would prove deceptive and disillusioning. People, objects, even places were often not what they seemed at all. A private girls school, so serene and Eden-like, could be a surprising setting for cold-blooded crime. History, too, was often misleading and inaccurate, accusing the innocent and pardoning the guilty—sometimes in fact making martyrs of them. Above all, these are the novels of a lonely woman, unable to communicate easily except through her writings. The final irony of her life is that she is remembered not for the dramas she loved, but for "her yearly knitting," the mystery novels she scorned.

VIII   *Flaws and Strengths*

Of all the critical comments on Tey, the most frequent concerns her weak plotting. There is no doubt that in the early detective novels, plotting is not her strongest point. Coincidences are suspiciously convenient; often the solution to the crime depends more on the weakness and ultimate confession of the killer than on the brilliance of the detective. Foreshadowing is sometimes clumsy, particularly in the biography *Claverhouse.* Descriptions are sometimes over-long, as in *The Man in the Queue,* and the probings into Grant's soul are often tedious in the earlier works.

However, Tey's ability with dialogue sets her among the masters of the genre. She avoids dull language and creates a natural and believable dialogue between interesting and developed characters. The minor characters in particular are realistic, reasonable, and memorable. Tey does not limit her character analysis to motive and passions, but explores tendencies, propensities, and states of mind. The background and the events in which the characters become involved are at least theoretically possible and far from absurd. She creates, in fact, not a puzzle of crime, but a puzzle of character and a drama of psychological conflicts.

IX Tey and Her Contemporaries

Studied in terms of contemporary women writers such as Dorothy L. Sayers, Margery Allingham, and Ngaio Marsh, Tey fits into the best of their traditions. Like Sayers, she sets her mysteries against a generally commonplace background which would not in itself be dramatic—a school, for example, or a horse farm. While detection is not always at the center of Tey novels, her detective Inspector Grant is undeniably a "gentleman" detective like Marsh's Inspector Alleyn. He is stable, staid, pure, unbribable, moralistic, and—in Grant's case—overly sensitive and conscience-ridden. The detective has a taste for fine food: Wimsey's knowledge of wine is famous, and Tey has Marta and Grant acknowledge his own good taste in *To Love* and *Be Wise* and *The Singing Sands.*

Often, in these mystery novels, there is something mysterious about the victim, for example, in Sayers' *Unnatural Death* and Tey's *The Man in the Queue.* Occasionally, as in *Whose Body?* and *A Shilling For Candles,* the identity of the corpse is unknown. Violence is bloodless and essentially unimportant, occurring mostly offstage, as it were. There is no unnecessary cruelty, and the victim is seldom seen alive. There exists none of the everyday worries of money, bombs, war, inflation, or what to serve for dinner. Moreover, Grant is not unique in his health problems. Wimsey's emotional problems following the war are often alluded to in the Sayers novels.

Most of the other writers, unlike Tey, insist on at least one murder per novel. Since general order prevails in the world of detective fiction, the good do not suffer for long and the bad are always punished. However, occasionally a murderer is slightly mad like Mrs. Wallis in *The Man in the Queue*. Madness, however, like violence, is never offensive, but often exists and is always discovered. Sometimes detection is used not to discover the identity of the criminal, since that is known, but to prove his guilt. This is true both in Sayers' *Unnatural Death* and Tey's *The Franchise Affair*.

Tey, however, does approach the mystery and detective novel with some differences. In three of her novels, *The Franchise Affair, Brat Farrar,* and *To Love and Be Wise,* fraud is the primary crime. And only in *The Franchise Affair* is it punished publicly. In *The Daughter of Time* Tey uses a device never successfully approached by her contemporaries. She solves an historical mystery without directly portraying any of the characters involved. It is this ability to create suspense without action, and to establish memorable characters with realistic dialogue that accounts for Tey's continuing popularity. She spans the worlds of the vicarage and the hard, city detective, creating, especially in her later works, compelling novels of personal conflict and mental self-torture. She provides the reader and herself with a bastion of predictability and surety in a world where all appearances deceive and disillusionment is common currency.

Notes and References

Chapter One

1. *Twentieth Century Authors* (Chicago, Illinois: Gayle Research Corp., 1954), pp. 620-21.
2. *Who's Who* (New York: St. Martins Press, 1948), pp. 695-96.
3. Sir John Gielgud, "Foreword," *Plays by Gordon Daviot* (London: Peter Davies, 1953), p. ix.
4. *Twentieth Century Authors*, p. 620.
5. Gielgud, p. x.
6. *To Love and Be Wise* (New York: The Macmillan Co., 1950; reprint, New York: Berkley Medallion Books, 1971), pp. 154-55.
7. *To Love and Be Wise*, p. 155.

Chapter Two

1. *Plays by Gordon Daviot*, Vol. 1 (London: Peter Davies, 1953), p. 235.
2. Ibid. Vol. II, p. 211.

Chapter Three

1. Review of *Expensive Halo, New York Times*, October 25, 1931, p. 24.
2. Ibid.
3. *Claverhouse* (London: Collins, 1937), p. 90.
4. *The Privateer* (New York: The Macmillan Co.., 1952), p. 269.
5. James Kelley, review of *The Privateer, New York Times*, August 24, 1952, p. 17.
6. Edward Fitzgerald, "Fiction Notes," review of *The Privateer, The Saturday Review*, September 6, 1952, p. 31.

Chapter Four

1. P. E. R. Review of *Man in the Queue, Boston Transcript*, September 21, 1929, p. 3.
2. Anon. Review of *Man in the Queue, New York Times*, July 28, 1929, p. 13.

3. S. S. Van Dine, "Twenty Rules for Writing Detective Stories," reprinted in *Writing Detective and Mystey Fiction*, A. S. Burack, ed. (Boston, 1967), p. 51.

4. Van Dine, p. 51.

5. Raymond Chandler, "The Simple Art of Murder," *The Simple Art of Murder* (New York, 1950; reprint, 1972), pp. 20-21.

6. *Man in the Queue*, (New York: The Macmillan Co., 1929; reprint, Berkley Medallion Books, 1962), pp. 6-7. Further references will be given in the text.

Chapter Five

1. Scott Sutherland, *Blood in Their Ink* (London, 1953), p. 108.

2. *A Shilling for Candles* (New York: The Macmillan Co., 1936; reprint, Berkley Medallion Books, March, 1960), p. 12. Further references will be given in the text.

Chapter Six

1. *Miss Pym Disposes* (New York: The Macmillan Co., 1947; reprint, Berkley Medallion Books, July, 1971), p. 7. Further references will be given in the text.

2. W. H. Auden, "The Guilty Vicarage," *The Dyer's Hand* (New York, 1948). Reprinted in *A Mystery Reader: Stories of Detection, Adventure and Horror,* Nancy Ellen Talburt and Lyna Lee Montgomery, eds. (New York: Charles Scribner's Sons, 1975) pp. 208-14.

Chapter Seven

1. *Brat Farrar* (New York: The Macmillan Co., 1949; reprint, Berkley Medallion Books, April, 1971), p. 9. Further references will be given in the text.

2. Ralph Partridge, review of *Brat Farrar, New Statesman & Nation,* Vol. 38, November 5, 1949, p. 530.

3. Review of *Brat Farrar, New Yorker,* March 4, 1950, p. 92.

4. Anthony Boucher, review of *Brat Farrar, New York Times,* March 19, 1950, p. 34.

Chapter Eight

1. *The Franchise Affair* (New York: The Macmillan Co., 1949; reprint, Berkley Medallion Books, February, 1971), p. 11. Further references will be given in the text.

2. James Sandoe, review of *The Franchise Affair, Chicago Sun,* February 11, 1949, p. 14.

3. Will Cuppy, review of *The Franchise Affair, New York Herald Tribune Weekly Book Review*, February 13, 1949, p. 14.

4. Arther Machen, *The Canning Wonder* (London, 1925), p. v.

5. Ibid., p. 165.

6. Ibid., p. 81.

7. Ibid., p. 81.

Chapter Nine

1. *To Love and Be Wise* (New York: The Macmillan Co., 1950; reprint Berkley Medallion Books, September, 1971), p. 12. Further references will be given in the text.

2. W. H. Auden, "The Guilty Vicarage," in *A Mystery Reader*, Talburt and Montgomery, eds. (New York, 1975), pp. 208–14.

3. M. Hoakes, review of *To Love and Be Wise, The New York Times*, May 25, 1951, p. 18.

4. "Mystery and Adventure," review of *To Love and Be Wise, New York Herald Tribune Book Review*, April 18, 1951, p. 15

5. Earle F. Walbridge, review of *To Love and Be Wise, Library Journal*, Vol. 76, March 1, 1951, p. 407.

6. A review of *To Love and Be Wise, New Yorker*, Vol. 27, March 24, 1951, p. 51.

Chapter Ten

1. Review *Times* (London) *Literary Supplement*, August 31, 1951, p. 545.

2. Anthony Boucher, review of *The Daughter of Time, New York Times Book Review*, February 24, 1952, p. 31.

3. James Sandoe, "Mystery and Suspense," review of *The Daughter of Time, New York Herald*, February 24, 1952, p. 10.

4. Julian Symons, *Bloody Murder* (London, 1972), p. 155.

5. *The Daughter of Time* (New York: The Macmillan Co., 1951; reprint, Berkley Medallion Books, August, 1959), p. 10. Further references will be given in the text.

Chapter Eleven

1. *The Singing Sands* (New York: The Macmillan Co., 1952; reprint, Berkley Medallion Books, May, 1971), p. 5. Further references will be given in the text.

2. S. S. Van Dine, "Twenty Rules for Writing Detective Stories," in *Writing Detective and Mystery Fiction*, (Boston, 1967), p. 49.

3. Anthony Boucher, review of *The Singing Sands, New York Times*, May 17, 1953, p. 29.

4. *The Man in the Queue* (New York: The Macmillan Co., 1929;

reissued by Berkeley Medallion Books, December, 1962), p. 58.

5. Review of *The Singing Sands, Times* (London) *Literary Supplement*, September 26, 1952, p. 625.

6. James Sandoe, "Mystery and Suspense," review of *The Singing Sands, New York Herald*, June 28, 1953, p. 12.

7. Boucher, p. 29.

Chapter Twelve

1. Scott Sutherland, *Blood in Their Ink* (London, 1953), p. 80.
2. Ibid., p. 109.
3. Ibid., p. 109.
4. *Miss Pym Disposes,* p. 223.
5. Chandler, R. *The Simple Art of Murder* (New York, 1971), p. 20.
6. Ibid., pp 20–21.
7. *The Singing Sands,* p. 103.
8. *The Franchise Affair,* p. 188.
9. *Man in the Queue* (New York: Macmillan, 1929), p. 206.
10. *Franchise,* pp. 222–23.
11. *To Love and Be Wise* (New York: Macmillan, 1950), p. 250.
12. *The Singing Sands,* p. 199.

Selected Bibliography

PRIMARY SOURCES

1. As Josephine Tey

Brat Farrar. New York: The Macmillan Co., 1949. Reprint, New York: Berkley Medallion Books, April, 1971.
The Daughter of Time. New York: The Macmillan Co., 1951. Reprint, New York: Berkley Medallion Books, August, 1959.
The Franchise Affair. New York: The Macmillan Co., 1949. Reprint, New York: Berkley Medallion Books, February, 1971.
The Man in the Queue. New York: Berkley Medallion Books, December, 1962.
Miss Pym Disposes. New York: The Macmillan Co., 1947. Reprint, New York: Berkley Medallion Books, July, 1971.
A Shilling for Candles. New York: The Macmillan Co., 1936. Reprint, New York: Berkley Medallion Books, 1960.
The Singing Sands. New York: The Macmillan Co., 1952. Reprint, New York: Berkley Medallion Books, May, 1971.
To Love and Be Wise. New York: The Macmillan Co., 1950. Reprint, New York: Berkley Medallion Books, September, 1971.

2. As Gordon Daviot: Fiction

Claverhouse. London: Collins, 1937.
The Expensive Halo. New York: Appleton & Co., 1931.
Kif: An Unvarnished History. New York: Appleton & Co., 1929.
The Man in the Queue. New York: The Macmillan Co., 1929.
The Privateer. New York: The Macmillan Co., 1952.

3. As Gordon Daviot: Drama

The Balwhinnie Bomb. Plays of Gordon Daviot, Vol. 2. London: Peter Davies, 1954.
Barnharrow. Plays by Gordon Daviot, Vol. 3. London: Peter Davies, 1954.
Clarion Call. Leith Sands and Other Short Plays. London: Duckworth, 1946.

Cornelia. Plays of Gordon Daviot, Vol. 2. London: Peter Davies, 1954.

Dickon. Plays by Gordon Daviot, Vol. 1. London: Peter Davies, 1953.

Lady Charing is Cross. Plays by Gordon Daviot. Vol. 3. London: Peter Davies, 1954.

The Laughing Woman. London: Victor Gollancz, Ltd. 1934.

Leith Sands. Leith Sands and Other Short Plays. London: Duckworth, 1946.

The Little Dry Thorn. Plays by Gordon Daviot. Vol. 1. London: Peter Davies, 1953.

The Mother of Masé. Leith Sands and Other Short Plays. London: Duckworth, 1946.

Mrs. Fry Has a Visitor. Leith Sands and Other Short Plays: London: Duckworth, 1946.

Patria. Plays of Gordon Daviot. Vol. 2. London: Peter Davies, 1954.

The Pen of my Aunt. Plays of Gordon Daviot. Vol. 2. London: Peter Davies, 1954.

Plays by Gordon Daviot. 3 Vols. London: Peter Davies, 1953–1954.

The Pomp of Mr. Pomfret. Plays by Gordon Daviot. Vol. 2. London: Peter Davies, 1954.

The Princess Who Liked Cherry Pie. Plays of Gordon Daviot. Vol. 2. London: Peter Davies, 1954.

Queen of Scots. London: Victor Gollancz, Ltd., 1934.

Rahab. Leith Sands and Other Short Plays. London: Duckworth, 1946.

Reckoning. Plays by Gordon Daviot. Vol. 3. London: Peter Davies, 1954.

Remember Caesar. Leith Sands and Other Short Plays. London: Duckworth, 1946.

Richard of Bordeaux. Boston: Little, Brown, and Co., July, 1933.

Sara. Leith Sands and Other Short Plays. London: Duckworth, 1946.

The Staff Room. Plays by Gordon Daviot. Vol. 3. London: Peter Davies, 1954.

The Stars Bow Down. London: Duckworth, 1939.

Sweet Coz. Plays by Gordon Daviot. Vol. 3. London: Peter Davies, 1954.

Three Mrs. Madderleys. Leith Sands and Other Short Plays. London: Duckworth 1946.

Valerius. Plays by Gordon Daviot. Vol. 1. London: Peter Davies, 1953.

SECONDARY SOURCES

1. Significant Reviews of the Daviot Dramas

NATHAN, GEORGE JEAN. "Art of the Night." *Saturday Review*, November 4, 1936, p. 8. Poor review of *The Laughing Woman:* "In the way of drama it is rich."

YOUNG, STARK. "Three Serious Plays." *New Republic*, March 14, 1934, p. 132. Negative review of the New York Production of *Richard III* complaining of an excess of verbiage and poor acting.

2. Significant Reviews of The Daviot Novels

ANON. Review of *Expensive Halo, New York Times*, October 25, 1931, p. 24. A penetratingly harsh review referring to "literary ventriloquism" and "skilled plot."

FITZGERALD, EDU. "Fiction Notes." *Saturday Review*, September 6, 1952, p. 31. A very favorable review of *The Privateer*, calls the novel "a fast yarn that has plenty of color and action and is told with the effortless skill for which she was noted."

KELLY, JAMES. "The Privateer." *New York Times*, August 24, 1952, p. 17. Calls *The Privateer* "a sparking good yarn."

3. Significant Reviews of the Tey Novels
The Man in The Queue

ANON. "New Mystery Stories." *New York Times*, July 28, 1929, p. 13. "Judicious pruning would have made the story much more readable."

ANON. *Times* [London] *Literary Supplement*, July 11, 1929, p. 561. A brief and succinct plot summary.

BOUCHER, ANTHONY. "Report on Criminals at Large." *New York Times*, September 16, 1953, p. 10. A good and incisive review; "extraordinarily ahead of its time."

P.E.R. *Boston Transcript*, September 21, 1929, p. 3.

SANDOE, JAMES. "Mystery & Suspense." *New York Herald Tribune Book Review*, September 6, 1953, p. 8. Very favorable, calling it "a member of an admirable company."

A Shilling for Candles

BOUCHER, ANTHONY. "Report on Criminals at Large." *New York Times Book Review*, April 18, 1954, p. 23. Favorable. Calls the book "a joy absolute."

SANDOE, JAMES. "Mystery & Suspense." *New York Herald Tribune Book Review*. March 28, 1954, p. 12. "The special charm of Miss Tey's tales lies in her capacity to keep one amused."

The Franchise Affair

CUPPY, WILL. *New York Herald Tribune Weekly Book Review*. February 13, 1949, p. 14. Highly recommends the well-written novel.

DAVIS, DOROTHY SALISBURY. "On Josephine Tey." *New Republic* September 20, 1954, pp. 17–18. Review of *Three by Tey,* a reissue of *The Franchise Affair, Brat Farrar,* and *Miss Pym Disposes.* One characteristic that most distinguished Tey's work "was her power to evoke character, atmosphere, more by conversation."

SANDOE, JAMES. *The Chicago Sun.* February 11, 1949, p. 14 Describes the book's "solid merits" as a detective novel.

Brat Farrar

ANON. "Mystery and Crime." *New Yorker,* March 4, 1952, p. 91. Very favorable: "The best of its kind in many months."

ANON. "Mystery and Adventure." *New York Herald Tribune Book Review,* March 26, 1950, p. 19. Ambivalent; "far from credible," but with "quiet wit and [a] sense of characterization."

BOUCHER, ANTHONY. "Heir Apparent." *New York Times,* March 19, 1950, p. 34. "The ingenious plot is suspensefully unfolded."

PARTRIDGE, RALPH. *New Statesman & Nation,* Vol. 38, November 5, 1949, p. 530. Terms Tey's "wonderful gift for portraying impostors" makes the book memorable.

To Love and Be Wise

ANON. *New Yorker,* Vol. 27, March 24, 1951, p. 108. A derogatory review.

ANON. "Mystery and Adventure." *New York Herald Tribune Book Review,* April 8, 1951, p. 15. A mixed review: "a smattering of that irony does crop up in this newest novel which poses a rather slim story but does it pleasantly."

HOAKES, M. *New York Times.* May 25, 1951, p. 18. Felt that Miss Tey could do better.

WALBRIDGE, EARLE F. *The Library Journal,* Vol. 76, March 1, 1951, p. 407. Negative review insisting "credulity and mystery collapse."

The Daughter of Time

ANON. *Times* [London] *Literary Supplement.* August 31, 1951, p. 545. A favorable review, brushing aside the problem of her approach of whitewashing the rogue.

ANON. "Mystery and Crime." *New Yorker,* February 23, 1952, p. 112.
  Favorable review, terming the work "original and absorbing."
BOUCHER, ANTHONY. "Reports on Criminals at Large." *New York Times
  Book Review,* February 24, 1952, p. 31. One of the "permanent
  classic(s)".
SANDOE, JAMES. "Mystery and Suspense." *New York Herald Tribune,*
  February 24, 1952, p. 10. *The Daughter of Time* "especially
  satisfying . . . gains its delight principally in the warmth of
  discernment of her observation of people and things."

The Singing Sands

ANON. *Times* [London] *Literary Supplement.* September 26, 1952. p.
  625. Negative review complaining of the slow start and lack of
  significant detection in the conclusion.
BOUCHER, ANTHONY. "Criminals at Large." *New York Times,* May 17,
  1953, p. 29. "Warm, beautifully written, and insistently readable
  book."
SANDOE, JAMES. "Mystery & Suspense." *New York Herald Tribune Book
  Review,* June 28, 1953, p. 12. Calls the book "a sound & solid
  acquaintance."

General Studies & Sources of Detective Fiction

AUDEN, W. H. "The Guilty Vicarage." *Dyer's Hand and Other Essays.*
  New York: Vintage Books, 1968, pp. 146–58. Classic study of form
  in the Golden Age Novel.
BARZUN, JACQUES. "Not 'Whodunit' But 'How?'," *Saturday Review,*
  November 4, 1944, pp. 9–11. Interesting and careful definition of
  styles and types of detective fiction.
BARZUN, JACQUES, and TAYLOR, WENDELL HERTIG. *A Catalogue of Crime.*
  New York: Harper & Row, 1971. An invaluable reference work
  including a detailed study of types of detective fiction as well as an
  extensive annotated bibliography of novels, short stories, plays,
  studies, true crime, Holmesiana, and ghost stories.
BOCCA, GEOFFREY. *The Life and Death of Sir Harry Oakes.* Garden City,
  N. Y.: Doubleday & Co., 1959. Carefully researched biography of
  the mysteriously murdered Sir Harry Oakes.
BURACK, A. S., ed. *Writing Detective and Mystery fiction.* Boston: The
  Writer, Inc., 1967. A collection of essays on the history and
  techniques of detective fiction, including "Twenty Rules for
  Writing Detective Stories" by S. S. Van Dine and "The Rules of the
  Game" by H. Haycraft.

CHANDLER, RAYMOND. "The Simple Art of Murder." In *The Simple Art of Murder*. New York: Houghton Mifflin, 1950. Reprint, New York. Ballantine Books, Inc., 1972, pp. 1–21. Originally published in the *Atlantic Monthly*, December, 1944, this essay defines the "hard-boiled dick."

HAYCRAFT, HOWARD, ed. *The Art of The Mystery Story*. New York: Grosset & Dunlap, 1946. A comprehensive collection of essays including criticism, rules, advice on writing and collecting, and surmises about the future of detective writing. Among the works included are essays by Dorothy L. Sayers, Joseph Wood Krutch, Anthony Boucher, and Edmund Wilson.

———. ed. *Murder for Pleasure*. New York: Biblo and Tannen, 1968. A careful study of the history of the genre as well as significant authors; includes the interesting and useful chronological listing of "cornerstones" in Detection-Crime-Mystery fiction.

MACHEN, ARTHUR. *The Canning Wonder*. London: Chatto & Windus, 1925. A study of the recorded evidence in the Canning case with a few conjectures as to motivations of Canning and her witnesses.

MURCH, A. F. *The Development of The Detective Novel*. New York: Greenwood Press, 1968. A history of detective fiction through the Golen Age with a useful, though somewhat dated bibliography.

NEVINS, FRANCIS M., Jr., ed. *The Mystery Writer's Art*. Bowling Green, Ohio: Bowling Green University Popular Press, 1970. A collection of modern essays on detective fiction. Contains the J. Barzun article "Detection and The Literary Art."

PLATRUCK, KENNETH B. *Great Mysteries of History*. New York: Harper & Row, 1971. A collection of historical mysteries some of which have been successfully fictionalized.

SAYERS, DOROTHY L. "Aristotle on Detective Fiction." In *Unpopular Opinions*. London: Victor Gollancz, Ltd., 1946. A written version of the 1935 lecture in which Sayers, partly tongue in cheek, insists that Aristotle initially set down the rules for detective fiction.

———. ed., *The Omnibus of Crime*. New York: Payson & Clarke, 1928. A collection of the most influential short stories in detective fiction prefaced by a detailed account of the development of the genre; a classic.

SUTHERLAND, SCOTT. *Blood in their Ink*. London: Stanley Paul & Co., 1953. A comprehensive study of the history of detective fiction, accompanied by an extremely useful and interesting classification of techniques. Marred only by the author's somewhat bizarre author and plot preferences.

SYMONS, JULIAN. *Bloody Murder, From the Detective story to the Crime Novel: A History*. London: Faber and Faber, 1972. The most complete history of detective fiction, marred only by the author's personal prejudices. "It is a striking confirmation of the decay in the classical form that the only post-war writer thought by Haycraft worthy to enter the canon was Elizabeth Mackintosh . . ." (p. 154).

TALBURT, NANCY ELLEN, and MONTGOMERY, LYNA LEE, eds. *A Mystery Reader: Stories of Detection, Adventure and Horror.* New York: Charles Scribner's Sons, 1975. An admirable collection of short stories and some essays on detective fiction.

THOMSON, H. DOUGLAS. *Masters of Mystery.* Folcroft, Pa.: Folcroft, 1970. A careful, intensive study of types of detective fiction and techniques of some significant authors.

VAN DINE, S. S. "Twenty Rules for Writing Detective Stories." In *Writing Detective and Mystery Fiction,* A. S. Burack, ed. Boston: The Writer, Inc., 1967. Pp. 49–54. Twenty rules summing up the technique and approach of the Golden Age.

WEEKS, R. W. *The Historian as Detective.* New York: Harper & Row, 1968. A collection of essays analyzing the use of detection techniques in the study of history.

Index

196